INTERNATIONAL TRUCK
Color History

Tom Brownell and Patrick W. Ertel

MBI Publishing Company

First published in 1997 by MBI Publishing Company, PO Box 1, 729 Prospect Avenue, Osceola, WI 54020-0001 USA

MBI Publishing Company books are also available at discounts in bulk quantity for industrial or sales-promotional use. For details write to Special Sales Manager at Motorbooks International Wholesalers & Distributors, 729 Prospect Avenue, PO Box 1, Osceola, WI 54020-0001 USA.

Library of Congress Cataloging-in-Publication Data

Brownell, Tom.
       International truck color history / Tom Brownell & Patrick Ertel.
          p.   cm.
       Includes index.
       ISBN 0-7603-0361-4 (pbk. : alk. paper)
       1. IHC trucks—Pictorial works. 2. IHC trucks—History.
       I. Ertel, Patrick W.   II. Title.
       TL230.5.I213B76   1997
       629.224—dc21   97-38057

On the front cover: International celebrated its 50th anniversary as a truck builder in 1957. The Golden Anniversary Special, a fancy 1957 A-100 pickup, was produced as a limited edition model. In addition to its two-tone paint scheme and bright trim, the pickup featured a smooth-sided box. This perfectly restored Golden Anniversary Special is owned by Glenn and Barbara Patch. *Dan Lyons*

On the frontispiece: Many International collectors find a ready symbiosis between old trucks and tractors. It's clear that George Mitchell enjoys both.

On the title page: International so completely redesigned its L models that about the only parts carried over from the preceding KB series were the hub caps (on the half-tons) and one of the three-speed transmissions. George Mitchell owns this beautifully restored 1951 L 110 example.

On the back cover: Besides styling, the D series brought many important changes. Cabs were now of all-steel construction for greater strength and durability. Deeper door windows gave more glass area, and the windows now had rounded corners to match the contours of the cab. The cargo box on pickup models had reinforcing ribs on the sides, and the stake pockets were built into the box sides, rather than being tack-welded on, as had formerly been the case. This 1939 D-2 is owned by George Schroyer.

On the back cover, inset: Differences between earlier and later Metro models included parking lights placed below the headlights, addition of the IH insignia to the grille, and a painted rather than chromed front bumper. This 1953 RM 150 Metro belongs to George Mitchell.

Printed in Hong Kong

CONTENTS

chapter one

ORIGINS:
International Harvester, as "Down Home" as the Family Farm

The farm equipment and truck builder known through most of this century as International Harvester (IH) had its origins in two separate companies: McCormick Harvesting Co. and Deering Harvester Co. The McCormick branch grew out of the McCormick reaper—a breakthrough in agricultural technology no less significant than the plow. Prior to the reaper Cyrus Hall McCormick demonstrated to a few farmer friends in July 1831, grain had been harvested by men mowing down the tall grassy stalks with scythes. The work was slow, requiring a small army of men with strong back and arm muscles to cut through the grain fields at harvest time. In his invitation for the demonstration, McCormick had claimed his reaper would cut through five to six acres in a day—many times as much as a good man with a sharp scythe could harvest. The machine beat McCormick's claim. Though they may have been impressed, the men watching the demonstration probably didn't realize that they had witnessed a history-making event. Agriculture would never be the same.

Within a few years, McCormick was building reapers in commercial quantities, and by 1870 production had reached 100,000 annually. In 1879, the McCormick Harvesting Machine Company was incorporated and with on-going improvements the McCormick reaper could now bundle as well as cut the stalks of grain.

The farm equipment and truck manufacturer known for nearly a century as International Harvester (now Navistar International) has a rich heritage that can be seen by visiting the company's Archives, located at Navistar International's corporate headquarters in downtown Chicago.

Meanwhile, a reaper that would also tie the grain in uniform bundles had been developed and patented by a young inventor named John F. Appleby. The machine was refined and manufacturing rights purchased by a company called Gammon & Deering. Soon sales of the Deering binder posed such strong competition for McCormick that a "Harvester War" developed—each company cutting prices to a razor-thin margin. Sales exploded and though both companies remained profitable, neither could amass the capital needed to exploit the rapidly expanding market. The logical solution, to seek a merger, occurred in July 1902, though by this time Cyrus McCormick had died with ownership of his company passing to stock holders. The merger that created International Harvester Co. was finalized in August 1902.

Since the merger had provided the new company with abundant capital, as well as managerial energy and engineering talent, International Harvester Co. quickly moved to live up to its name and develop the virtually untapped world-wide market for its products. In 1903 construction of a new plant was begun in Hamilton, Ontario. By 1905 the first European plant had been built at Norrkopping, Sweden, and in 1906 sales to Russia equaled the sum total of all McCormick's and Deering's export trade before the merger. In 1909 Germany was added to the list of countries where International Harvester had manufacturing plants, and soon afterward plants were opened in France and Russia.

The company began manufacturing tractors in 1906 and the Auto Buggy, International Harvester's first truck, appeared in 1907. Looking more like a horseless wagon than an automobile, the Auto Buggy headed International Harvester in a direction that would chart the company's future for nearly a century—as a manufacturer of trucks. That the Auto Buggy lacked resemblance to other early automobiles wasn't a mistake. The vehicle wasn't intended to haul people as much as it was to haul things. What International Harvester had decided to market was an early rendition of a truck. In the years to follow, the company's truck development would branch in two directions: light-duty trucks for delivery use and medium and heavy trucks for larger loads. The company's major areas, farm equipment, tractors, and trucks would develop along separate paths, but all would contribute to a corporate identity that fairly spelled farm as the company's middle name.

International Harvester began as a well-managed enterprise. For the first 10 years, Charles Deering and Cyrus H. McCormick (a family successor to the reaper's inventor, Cyrus Hall McCormick), and George W. Perkins of the Morgan banking interests managed the company's affairs. Among their accomplish-ments, this talented, experienced trio protected the company from stock speculators by a trust arrangement, under which only the directors had voting privileges. This established a climate of stability that enabled International Harvester to expand rapidly and aggressively into new markets. The widespread use of trucks in World War I and rapid recognition of the benefits of trucks by farmers and small businesses opened a market that IH moved into, first with its Auto Wagon, then with the Slope Hood models, followed by the hugely successful S series that made International a leader in the truck industry—a banner the company would proudly wave for the next half century.

Continued strong management kept International Harvester in a leadership position within its industry. Through the 1930s and 1940s, International trucks wore styling that was not only distinctive, but aesthetically very pleasing. The company's products continued to display excellent engineering that created strong bonds of buyer loyalty. In the 1950s, however, International's position among light truck buyers began to change. Faced with increasingly rapid restyling cycles caused by an intense marketing battle between Ford and GM, International chose to retrench, stretching styling intervals to nearly a decade. In the 1930s, in contrast, International brought its truck line through three complete styling cycles in less than nine years. Although its buyers remained faithful to the

International brand, the company's trucks (Scout excepted) failed to make significant inroads in a rapidly expanding market. Through the 1960s, International's light truck sales held steady at slightly over 48,000 units annually. But in 1965, the combined light truck sales of Ford and Chevrolet had reached nearly one million. On the sales charts, International was being lost in the dust. Even the popular Scout, which had broken all of International's previous sales records, settled into mediocre sales performance simultaneous with exploding sales figures set by Ford's Bronco and Chevrolet's Blazer. Something was clearly going wrong.

International's dropping first its light-truck line in 1975 and then the Scout in 1980 can be traced to four causes: 1) a long and bitter strike with resulting labor conflict that continues to this day; 2) turf battles between "big truck" and "light truck" management, which the big truck people won; 3) the location of International's dealerships, which, because they focused primarily on a farming clientele, were out of the heavy buyer traffic; and 4) lack of marketing attention toward women.

Unfortunately, the result of these and other problems led not only to International's shucking its light truck lines (the Scout's loss was especially significant, since the marque's talented designer Ted Ornas had developed a composite bodied successor that might well have led the company's revival in the strong off-road vehicle market), but

also losing its agricultural equipment business— and corporate name—to Case.

Today in the place of International Harvester we have Navistar International, a slimmer, more focused company, that has met sales success with its medium and heavy-duty truck lines. Navistar has found great acceptance among fleet buyers, and is competing in international markets. It is, however, plagued by issues facing many long-established companies seeking to sharpen their competitiveness in a business climate where change is the only constant. Navistar's challenges, razor-thin profit margins and high labor costs, will require management initiatives every bit as inventive as those employed by the company's founders and vision approaching that of Cyrus McCormick in inventing the reaper. But where challenges exist, there are also opportunities. For Navistar, some of these lie with International markets. At the time of this book's writing, the company is attempting to forge a partnership with one of the larger truck builders of Eastern Europe to supply engines for that company's medium and heavy-duty trucks. Partnerships of this nature may be one way for Navistar to meet its challenges while also penetrating previously inaccessible markets. The company has a proud heritage and a long distinguished history. We look forward to waving the Navistar banner as the company leads the U.S. truck manufacturing industry into the third millennium.

chapter two

EARLY TRUCKS:
"High Wheelers"
and Slope Hood Models

Like most other early automotive manufacturers, International didn't set out to build motorcars (or, more appropriately, from our point of view, motor trucks). International's entry in the "horseless carriage" business happened in a sort of roundabout, coincidental way. Most of the early automobile designers were tinkerers, men like Henry Ford and Ransom E. Olds. They possessed machinists' skills, meaning that they liked to take things apart to see how they worked, and they were fascinated by the gasoline-powered buggies (most of which had been imported from England, France, or Germany) that happened quite literally to cross their paths. Lacking cash, and none of the early automotive pioneers was a wealthy man, they knew that if they wanted to own a motor powered vehicle, they'd have to build it.

The tinkerer who led to International's becoming one of the very earliest companies to build gasoline-powered vehicles was Edward A. (E.A.) Johnson. This budding inventor first took employment with McCormick Harvesting Machine Co. in 1894 at the age of 18. By 1898, Johnson had built his first automobile. Although it looked much like Henry Ford's Quadracycle, which was completed in 1896, Johnson's self-powered buggy was quite different mechanically. Johnson's auto-buggy was chain-drive, whereas Ford's Quadracyle used a belt drive, and Johnson had adopted as his power source a McCormick stationary engine.

Using experience gained with his automobile, Johnson designed an auto-mower that McCormick displayed at the Paris Exposition of 1900—where the machine won a first prize.

What happened next was a set of events no one, and certainly not E. A. Johnson, could have predicted. In 1902, Johnson left McCormick to join the Keystone Co. of Rock Falls, Illinois. Like McCormick, Keystone was a manufacturer or agricultural equipment, and Johnson was hired to design a new line of hay and grain harvesting machines. But then in 1905, the newly formed International Harvester Co. purchased Keystone, and once again acquired the services of that young, talented design engineer, E. A. Johnson. The greater resources of International Harvester allowed Johnson the opportunity to pursue his dream—designing a buildable automotive product. Within weeks, he was at work on his Auto Buggy. It was approved for production in 1906, and the first examples were completed by the McCormick Works in Chicago by February 1907.

From the start, International's Auto Buggy enjoyed brisk sales, so brisk that by October of the same year, production was moved to a more spacious site at the Akron, Ohio, Works. Steady

> International built its Slope Hood trucks in four models, the H, F, G, and L, ranging in load capacity from 3/4-ton to 3-ton. All Slope Hood trucks shared the same basic water-cooled, overhead-valve four-cylinder engine. The example shown here is a 1-ton rated Model F owned by George Mitchell. The Model F was the second-largest seller in this series, with a sales total of 7,455 units.

With the Auto Wagon, International set in motion a nearly three-quarter-century tradition of building well-engineered light trucks. Today most surviving Auto Buggies and Auto Wagons are in museums, but some still remain in the hands of private collectors, and these can be seen and enjoyed at truck shows like the Antique Truck Club of America's annual gathering at Macungie, Pennsylvania.

sales continued and soon Auto Buggies were being completed at the "frantic" rate of about four a day for a production total of nearly 1,000 a year. The name Auto Buggy aptly describes these early vehicles. Not only were the wheels tall and buggy-like, even the seats were buggy-style. The engine's location underneath the body contributed to the buggy- like appearance.

Although International designed and built a few true cars with a forward-mounted engine, windshield, full fenders, and top, the company stayed true to its agricultural tradition. The Auto Buggy evolved into an Auto Wagon, which was mechanically the same but more buckboard-like in appearance, with a single two-person seat and a cargo area behind. As a side note, the cars were as innovative and advanced in their design as the Auto Wagons, in that the engine featured an overhead camshaft—a design feature that later would distinguish the mighty Duesenberg and much later would become commonplace.

International's early truck-type vehicles were given the nickname "High Wheelers" because of the tall wood-spoked wheels and narrow solid rubber tires that enabled these self-propelled cargo wagons to navigate the primitive rural roads. After a rain or during spring thaw, when dirt roads and farm lanes would be cut through with muddy ruts, the tall wheels and skinny tires would sink to the bottom of the mud, which might be a foot or more deep, finding traction on the more solid footing below. In these pioneering days, engine design had not progressed to the stage where traction could be gained by the vehicle's lunging itself against obstacles. Instead, an early Auto Buggy or Auto Wagon moved slowly through whatever morass lay in its path—and in those days before hard surface roads, "morass" is perhaps the best way to describe the trails a farm wagon might travel.

Since the easiest way to traverse a road cut deep with ruts is to follow in the path of the ruts, International built some of its Auto Buggies with wider wheel tracks for a regional match to the farm wagons. A 56-inch wheel track (distance between the wheels measured along the length of the axle) was standard, while the wide track Auto Buggy, designated the Model D, spaced the wheels 60 inches apart. The Model D was marketed in the rural South, where its wheel track matched that of tobacco and cotton wagons.

Perhaps the Auto Buggy/Auto Wagon's most novel feature was its two-cylinder opposed air-cooled engine which, along with the transmission and differential, was mounted on an angle-iron frame and located underneath the body. Two cooling fans, belt driven from the flywheel, drew air across the engine cylinders. Since the cylinders and head were cast as a single unit, as was typical in early engine designs, the cylinders had to be removed from the block to get at the pistons. The valves, which were in an "overhead" location, were set in cages that bolt to the cylinders. The rockers and pushrods were exposed (as was common with overhead valve engines in that day), while hairpin-style springs maintained valve tension. With a four-cycle design and a 5-inch bore and stroke, the engine produced 15 horsepower that allowed speeds up to 20 miles per hour.

Mounted beside the engine, a planetary transmission drove a primary chain that turned a jackshaft with chain sprockets on either end for powering the rear wheels. From a "who-built-it-first" perspective, it is interesting to note that International mounted the engine and transmission on its Auto Buggies and Auto Wagons transversely

While International used a two-cylinder air-cooled engine to power its Auto Buggies, with the introduction of the Auto Wagon, a water-cooled engine became available as an option. The air-cooled version carried an AW designation, while the water-cooled model was designated MW. Both air-cooled and water-cooled engines were mounted in the same location under the body and shared the same 5-inch bore and stroke. On water-cooled models, the radiator is in the traditional location at the front of the stubby hood. The Model MW Auto Wagon shown here is owned by Tom Dixon.

in the chassis. Today, nearly all domestic and imported front-wheel-drive cars and some light-duty trucks use this same transverse-mounted engine/transmission design.

Brakes of the external contracting type (with shoes contacting the outsides of the brake drums) were mounted only at the rear wheels. Because their moving parts are exposed to mud and moisture, external contracting brakes are not especially reliable, and even when the breaking mechanism functions properly, the size of the braking pads and drums on these early vehicles was quite small. However, this brake design was adequate for the very limited traffic (which was largely horses and wagons) and low speeds of the day.

Early automobiles lacked a standardized location for the steering wheel. Some placed the driver on the left, others on the right. Actually, the very earliest cars hadn't used steering wheels, but instead steered with a tiller, or simple lever like that used to control the rudder on a boat, that was usually reached from the center of the front seat. Even International's earliest Auto Buggies had used this tiller steering mechanism. Subsequent Auto Buggy/Auto Wagons placed the steering wheel on the vehicle's right side, the driver location found today in the United Kingdom, Australia, and Japan.

Although the nickname High Wheeler is commonly used in reference to any International Auto Buggies and Auto Wagons, not all models had wheels of the same height. On early models the wheel height is 40 inches in front and 44 inches in rear. In 1910, both sets of wheels were lowered two inches, making the new measurements 38 inches at the front and 42 inches on the rear.

As this profile shot of Dixon's Auto Wagon shows, early International trucks looked nearly identical to a horse-drawn wagon, minus the horse.

All Auto Buggies and Auto Wagons produced from 1907 to 1913 wore the familiar script IHC logo, displayed prominently in the front of the hood over the fake radiator. Remember, there's an air-cooled engine slung under the chassis of that IHC Auto Buggy or Auto Wagon, and the stubby hood and "radiator" are just decoys, making us think this truck has a traditional water-cooled engine. From 1913 until 1987, all International products carried the company's name, sometimes in combination with other logos like the famous Triple-Diamond. (In 1987, with the sale of the International Harvester name and farm equipment line to Case, the remaining truck manufacturing unit renamed itself Navistar International.)

With the Auto Wagon, International became the first company to build a multi-purpose light truck (what today we would call a pickup). In 1912, perhaps foreshadowing the eventual popularity of light truck, or maybe to draw its vehicle line closer to the company's agricultural base, the Auto Buggy was dropped and the Auto Wagon's name changed to Auto Truck. This was a good move.

Competition among car manufacturers was keen, and Henry Ford's spindly Model T had become an overnight sales success among America's farmers. But International's Auto Trucks also shared a measure of popularity. Many saw service on farms, others found work as delivery wagons for stores and shops, while some even carried the mail.

Also in 1912 a water-cooled engine became available as a buyer option. Both air- and water-cooled engines shared the same 5-inch bore and stroke. On water-cooled models, a real radiator was mounted at the front of the stubby front hood. To distinguish trucks fitted with the air-cooled engines from the water-cooled models, two model designations were introduced: AW (air) and MW (water).

In 1915, International introduced a longer, somewhat heavier duty (1,500-pound load capacity) Auto Truck called the Model E. With lower (36-inch) wheels, plus full fenders and a running board, these trucks had a slightly more modern look. Although narrow, hard rubber tires were standard equipment, a few Model Es were sold with

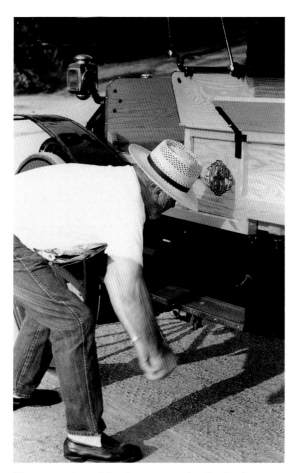

The engine's midship location under the body becomes apparent when the driver reaches for the starting crank.

Early automobiles lacked a standardized location for the steering wheel. On its Auto Buggies and Auto Wagons, International placed the steering wheel on the vehicle's right side, the driver location used today in the United Kingdom, Australia, and Japan.

pneumatic tires. Never a company to make drastic changes, International built the Model E simultaneous with the new Slope Hood models. The new trucks were at least a decade advanced technologically, and one would think that there would have been little contest in sales between the last of the "High Wheelers" and the new Slope Hood trucks, but nearly 1,500 Es found buyers. Quite possibly International recognized that rural folk tend to be conservative in their lifestyles and buying habits and once they have found a good product, they're likely to stay with it—even in the face of something altogether new and better.

The High Wheelers were sound products with a simple design. As the listing below shows, their sales, though respectable for the time, can't be called record-setting. In remembering the High Wheels, it's best to think of them as transition vehicles, making that all-important bridge between the horse drawn wagon and the yet-to-emerge pickup truck.

Auto Buggy - Auto Wagon Production

McCormick Works
  Auto Buggies
  Feb to Oct 1907   #s 101 to 200
Akron Works
  Auto Buggies
  Oct 1907 to March #s 201 to 2972
  1, 1910
  Auto Wagons
  1909 to 1912   #s 101A to 950B
  Auto Trucks
  1912 to 1916   #s 01AA to 1954E

A planetary transmission drove a primary chain that turned a jack-shaft with chain sprockets for powering the rear wheels. Though requiring high maintenance, chain drive proved more reliable on early vehicles than gear-driven rear axles, and the final drive ratio could be changed quite easily by installing larger or smaller chain sprockets.
Courtesy of This Old Truck *magazine*

1915–1923 Slope Hood Models

By 1915 America was beginning to make the transition from the horse and wagon to the motor truck. Looking at the "Slope Hood" International's funny, half-coffin looking hood with the radiator mounted behind, snuggled up against the driver, the obvious question arises—why that design? As soon as they moved the engine from underneath to up in front of the driver, practically every other truck maker (Mack, Stewart, Kelly Springfield, and International being the notable exceptions) put the radiator prominently at the head of the truck. As legend has it, there was a reason for International and its aforementioned companions locating the radiator *behind* the engine.

It seems there was lots of jealousy between teamsters (those who drove horses) and the new motorized truck operators. It didn't take a teamster with a nasty streak long to figure out that if his horse "accidentally" backed its wagon into the front of a motor truck (with the rear of the wagon smashing into the rather delicate radiator), the truck would be out of business—at least until the radiator could be repaired. Looking more closely at a Slope Hood International, you'll notice a fairly rugged cross member at the head of the frame. (On a Mack "Bulldog" this cross member is mammoth in proportion.) Presumably, when the teamster's wagon hit the front of an International Slope Hood it would strike the protecting cross member and little or no damage would be done. (When a horse drawn wagon hit the AC Mack "Bulldog's"

In another similarity with horse-drawn wagons, early motorized vehicles used kerosene lights, which provided more of a glow to help mark the vehicle's location than bright forward illumination. But nighttime travel was rare, speed approached a crawl, and traffic was virtually non-existent.

thick front casting, the damage probably occurred to the wagon.) So there's quite a bit of utility in that Slope Hood design, even if it did have the downside of radiating lots of heat into the cab. Of course in the wintertime, a driver could enjoy resting his feet on that toasty-warm firewall. The front opening hood also makes the engine as accessible as if it were sitting on an engine stand in the middle of your shop floor.

Although the E-type wagon would remain in production until 1917, in 1915, International introduced four new truck models that I have descriptively called "Slope Hood." These were the H, F, G, and L, the letters representing different load capacities from 3/4 ton to 3 tons. The four truck models shared the same basic water-cooled, overhead-valve

Externally, an air-cooled AW Auto Wagon appears nearly identical to an MW water-cooled model. This example is owned by Floyd Dancey. *Courtesy of* This Old Truck *magazine*

The lack of a filler cap on the top of the fake radiator provides a tell-tale giveaway to this Auto Wagon's air-cooled engine. *Courtesy of* This Old Truck *magazine*

On air-cooled Auto Wagons, cooling is accomplished by two fans that are belt-driven from the flywheel. Although extremely simple and looking rather crude, this cooling system worked. As can be seen, the valves are in an "overhead" location and activated by exposed pushrods. This engine produced 15 horsepower and allowed speeds up to 20 miles per hour. *Courtesy of* This Old Truck *magazine*

Above and right: The before and after photos of a restoration project serve not only as evidence of the restorer's skills, but also give admirers a glimpse of the transformation process. The Slope Hood International shown in these photos was skillfully and artfully restored by Winross Restorations of Newark, New York. *Winross Restorations*

In this under-chassis view, both the primary chain from the transmission and secondary chain to the rear wheel sprocket can be seen. On early vehicles, only the rear wheels had brakes.

four-cylinder engine, though different displacements were created by varying the size of the engine bore. (Engines in the Slope Hood series shared a common stroke of 5 1/4 inches, but had different bores ranging from 3 1/2 to 4 1/4 inches, depending on the truck's job rating.) All models also shared the same three-speed gearbox and used live rear axles.

Oddly, the Slope Hood model designations don't line up with the truck's load ratings. The logical sequence would be F G H L. Instead Model H was the new light duty entry with a load rating of 1,500 pounds, or 3/4 ton. The Model F had a 1-ton rating. Somewhat later International introduced a Model K with a 1 1/2-ton rating, followed by the Model G, a 2-ton truck. The 3 1/2-ton rated Model L represented International's heavy hauler.

From a sales standpoint, the Model G proved most popular, with 11,000 sold over the Slope Hood series' eight-year run. The Model F placed second with a sales total of 7,455. The Model H proved a modest sales success with slightly under 5,700 finding buyers. Sales for all Slope Hood models during their eight-year production totaled 32,000. While these figures were a shadow of the number of trucks International Harvester would build in the future, they spelled the end for the horse and wagon.

Another sign of the horse's replacement, on June 14, 1916, an F-Model International became the first

truck to climb Pike's Peak. The elapsed time isn't reported. The issue in this event wasn't speed; the challenge was endurance. The fact that a truck could climb all the way to top of one of the Continental United States' highest mountains spoke for what was most important—the truck's stamina. Early trucks weren't fast in today's sense (the Model L had its speed limited by a governor to 12 miles per hour, while the Model G traveled only slightly faster at 13 3/4)miles per hour), but they could deliver a load lots faster than a horse, and unlike a horse they didn't need to rest.

Unless the buyer specified otherwise, the Slope Hood truck he purchased rode on solid rubber tires. But pneumatic tires were available at extra cost on all models except the 3 1/2-ton L. The improved ride, increased speed, and better traction offered by pneumatic tires was one of the factors to the Slope Hood trucks' sales success—particularly since some competitors' trucks were fitted only with solid rub-

ber. As another improvement, Slope Hood trucks transferred power to the rear wheels via a live rear axle. Earlier International trucks had used chain drive, as did most trucks of the period. By using a gear-driven rear axle, International freed operators of time consuming chain maintenance, as well as the noisy sound of the whirring chains. International's long experience in building agricultural equipment and the knowledge of metals that could withstand the twisting forces of starting out under a load made the gear driven axle possible.

Improvements also occurred in braking and electrical equipment. Internal expanding brakes increased the trucks' stopping power and electric lights and an electric starter could be fitted as optional equipment. Gas lamps and crank starting were standard. An engine-driven magneto provided ignition voltage. The only instrument on the vertical dashboard was a fuel gauge.

Slope Hood Trucks Today

Any Slope Hood truck is a rarity that attracts attention, not just because of its senior status, but also because of the distinctive hood design and radiator location. Historically, Slope Hood trucks warrant collector interest because they represent the link between early buggy-style transport and the more versatile models that followed. Because the cabs and bodies were generally made of wood and could be from a variety of designs, restorers often use illustrations from catalogs, or patterns taken from another restored truck, in re-creating the usually badly deteriorated wooden body. So there's lots of room for creativity in deciding what appearance a restored Slope Hood International truck should take.

If you locate a Slope Hood International, it's more likely to be a Model G or its later Model 61 equivalent. The Model H, which had roughly half the G's sale and would be pickup sized by today's standards, is perhaps the most attractive from a collector standpoint—not only because of its proportions, but also because it can be displayed at the growing number of car shows that include a light truck class.

It's quite a novelty, and somewhat of a challenge, to drive an early truck. If starting is by crank, one has to get the hang of setting the spark, choke, and gas for the engine to fire on one or two pulls of the crank. Then there's the hand throttle to coordinate with the clutch and gear shifting—and the two-wheel brakes certainly aren't designed for twenty-first century city traffic. Archaic as they may seem, the long-forgotten driving patterns that we learn are part of the fun of old truck ownership.

For the most part, cab and cargo bodies were built by outside suppliers. Cab and body types could, and did, take practically any form—from an open cab consisting of little more than a windshield and buckboard-style seat to a fully enclosed wooden cab, and from a simple platform or stake body to fully enclosed delivery bodies, all built to suit the buyer's needs and pocketbook. With pneumatic tires, trucks could now be used year-round (hard rubber tires had two problems in snow or wet pavement: they lacked tread and didn't spread out on the bottom as do pneumatic tires). As a result, open-style cabs were generally provided with canopy tops and side curtains to give drivers a degree of protection from the weather.

In 1921, numbers replaced the letters, so that the Model H became the Model 21; the F became the 31; the G became the 61; and the L became the 101. As can be seen, the numbers now ran in sequence with the load capacity—but why, you may ask, were there such wide gaps between the numbers? Why not, for example, follow Model 21 and 31 with 41 and 51? There was a reason, which goes like this. The Model 21 (H) had a 1-ton (2,000-pound) rating (thus 21); the 31 (F), a 1 1/2-ton (3,000-pound) rating (thus 31); the 61 (G), a 3-ton (6,000-pound) rating (thus 61); and the 101 (L), a whopping 5-ton (10,000-pound) rating (thus 101). On some trucks, front-mounted radiators were now available, as were an additional set of rear booster springs. By the 1920s, enclosed cabs were becoming more common.

A reason given for International's mounting the radiator behind the engine on its Slope Hood trucks was the radiator's vulnerability in the event of a front-end collision. Such collisions could occur quite easily if an irate teamster decided to back his wagon into an approaching truck, blaming the accident on the truck's having frightened his horses, but also putting the offending truck out of business, at least temporarily.

The controls on a Slope Hood truck operated in the conventional fashion, with the spark manually retarded or advanced by moving a lever mounted on the steering wheel and the gearshift moving in a standard three-speed H pattern.

Electric lights were not yet standard equipment.

One of the more novel engine features of a Slope Hood International truck is the horizontal shaft that drives both the water pump and distributor. While the fan is mounted at the rear of the engine, the water pump drives from the front.

chapter three

1921-1929 S SERIES:
International Brings Speed
to Truck Buyers

In 1922 IHC purchased the Champion Farm Equipment Company, located in Springfield, Ohio. Production demands had already outstripped the company's Akron, Ohio, and Chicago manufacturing facilities, and in 1923 International moved the light-duty segment of its truck production to the newly acquired Springfield, Ohio, plant. The trucks emerging from the Springfield plant would represent an entirely redesigned truck series, called the S Model, that would meet changing demands of the truck market—namely higher speeds and greater versatility. The S series' success would make International one of the major players in the expanding truck industry.

Automotive engineers say that designing a successful new model vehicle is like trying to hit a moving target. The competition and the public's expectations are constantly changing. The challenge is to best the competition while providing the public with what it hasn't quite realized it wants. With its S series, International hit the moving target right on the bull's eye. Here was a truck that set a standard for its day and incorporated features that would soon become standard in the trucking industry, including pneumatic tires, electrical lighting, a self-starter, generator, battery, and horn. The sales figures speak for themselves: a total of 168,000 S-model trucks and derivatives were built in this series' seven-year production run.

Popular as the S series proved to be, it was launched at a precarious time. A study of business

> While the headlights on the early S models are positioned in the usual location between the radiator shell and front fenders, on later models the headlights were mounted on the cowl—an easy recognition feature.

cycles shows that a wartime boom is usually followed by a peacetime bust, and bust is what happened to the U.S. economy shortly after the end of World War I. The recession that followed the 1919 armistice was short but sharp. During this period, numerous businesses (included newly established auto and truck manufacturers) failed. Rather than simply adopt a "weather the storm" business policy, International used its new, highly competitive S-model trucks to open markets. As part of this scheme, the company sold bright red, attention-getting S models to its dealers at reduced price for use as service trucks. While these so-called "Red Babies" were out making service calls, delivering stationary engines and other equipment to farmers, they quickly caught prospective buyers' eyes. Today these "Red Baby" service trucks are among the rarer of S models and are sought by collectors for both their distinctive appearance and historical role in launching this popular series.

The initial S model was a light-duty 3/4-ton truck powered by a Lycoming four-cylinder engine. The truck's 35 horsepower allowed highway speeds of 25–30 miles per hour—certainly no threat to posted speed limits, but faster than the chain-driven trucks that still predominated. Although speed wasn't top on a buyer's list of priorities, common sense says that a truck with a cruising speed of 30 miles per hour can be more productive than one that pokes along at 15 miles per hour, particularly on longer hauls.

International's S series appeared just as the nation was experiencing a short, but sharp, depression. To attract buyers' attention to the new, improved line of trucks, dealers were urged to purchase service trucks, painted an attention-getting bright red, at a substantially reduced price. Called "Red Babies," these service trucks are among the rarer S models and are prized by collectors.

Even though International used its S-model trucks' faster speeds as a selling point in its ads, the S didn't stand for Speed, and the early S models aren't to be confused with the Speed trucks that appear later in this series. What differentiated the Speed trucks was auxiliary gearing that gave six forward speeds—hence their name Six Speed Special. The standard S model had a three-speed transmission that the driver shifted by working what was called a "multiple disk" clutch. A more complex and quirkier mechanism than the more common friction clutch, the multiple disk design was thought at the time to give superior longevity, something important in a working vehicle. In fact, reliability seems built into the S model's design. As one example, rather than drive the generator and water pump with a belt, as is common on engines even today, the Lycoming engines used by International featured a gear-driven generator, which, in turn, drove the water pump, which was mounted on the side of the engine between the generator and starter. With no belt to break, the operator of an S-model truck had one less reason to be let down on the job. Another example of International's engineering in reliability is the use of an air cleaner to prevent dirt and dust from being sucked into the engine. Two types of air cleaners can be found on S-series trucks. The earlier type is a simple tin canister with an internal baf-

fle that causes the air to change direction 180 degrees before entering the carburetor. The later cleaner is an "air-maze" type, which used a wire mesh to trap dust and other airborne particles. Without an air cleaner, dirt sucked directly into an open carburetor can score the cylinder walls, and dust inhaled into the engine while driving on dirt roads causes cylinder wall wear. Both conditions dramatically shorten engine life.

In 1923 International boosted the S model's load rating to 1 ton. Few changes are apparent between the early models of this series. The 3/4-ton load rating returned in 1924 with the introduction of a Special Delivery model. This truck, with its angular, enclosed wooden body, expanded International's market to businesses such as bakeries and dairies that needed a lighter duty delivery vehicle. Along with standard S-model features such as electric lighting and self-starter, the Special Delivery also offered options such as full length running boards and a nickel-plated radiator shell. The plated radiator shell gave a more up-scale look, which appealed to businesses whose trucks would have visibility with the public. The Special Delivery was built on a 116-inch wheelbase (early S trucks were offered on either a 115-inch or 124-inch wheelbase) and used a four-cylinder Waukesha engine of 143.9 cubic inches.

For 1925, the S line expanded with two new models, the SD and SL. Initially these trucks were rated at 1 ton, but were up-rated to 1 1/2 tons for 1926 and could even be ordered in tractor-trailer configurations. Like the standard S, the SD and SL models were equipped with Lycoming engines. In 1926, the S line expanded again with several new models. Load ratings on S-series trucks now reached 2 tons. The S-line models now carried designations S-24, S-26, SD-34, SD-36, SL-34, SL-36, SD-44, SD-46, SF-44, and SF-46. Models ending with a four were equipped with four-cylinder engines while models ending with a six featured six-cylinder Lycoming powerplants. Four-speed transmissions were now optional and the extra gearing was quite popular in heavier duty SF (2-ton rated) trucks. On S-24 and S-26 models (and perhaps others) a small compressor driven from the transmission provided compressed air for on-the-road tire repairs.

On S-model trucks, the weight, model, and serial number information is printed on a nameplate normally located on the right side of the cowl, just forward of the door, and just above the splash apron. This plate does not indicate the year of manufacture. It was common practice at the time for dealers to set the manufacturing date based on

When Ferris State University in Big Rapids, Michigan, acquired its 1927 S model, the odometer showed less than 100 miles. The truck was so well preserved that the factory chalk marks and assembly tags still showed on the chassis.

when the vehicle was sold. Consequently, a truck built near the end of 1923, but which sat in a dealer's inventory until 1924, would be dated a 1924 production year vehicle for registration and licensing purposes. The most likely tip-off to a vehicle's having been post-dated is the existence of features discontinued in the supposed year of manufacture. Serial or engine number lists by production year can also help accurately establish a vehicle's manufacture date when these lists are available.

By 1924 International was discontinuing the use of its older IHC emblem and trademark. Earlier, this familiar emblem had been stamped on the rear spring hangers of some trucks. The trademark continued to appear on spark plugs and other proprietary items. The International name, which was now being used as the identifying trademark,

better represented a company that was becoming one of the leading makers of light and medium duty trucks and whose products were now being sold all over the world. Besides its over 1,500 dealerships in the United States, International was aggressively pursuing the Canadian market. By 1928, its plant in Chatham, Ontario, Canada, which initially built both trucks and tractors, was solely producing trucks.

In keeping with the change of logo, the International name was printed low on the body sill behind the cab doors. This was not the only identifying marker. The radiator shell carried a triple diamond emblem overwritten with the International name, and the name and triple diamond insignia was embossed on the side of the engine block. "International" can be seen stamped in full-length

Enclosed cabs offered on S-model trucks were constructed largely of wood, with the result that a rotted cab can become the most challenging part of restoring an early truck.

When the S series was introduced, trucks were still something of a novelty, so International pitched its ads, not toward the advantages of its S models over competitors' trucks, but over a horse and wagon.

running boards, and the International name even appears on the rear axle banjo. On some models, International nameplates were attached to the sides of the hood. When fresh from the factory, an International sticker with the company's Chicago address was attached to the rear cross member. It's unlikely that this sticker will still be seen on most surviving S models, but the factory sticker in fact remains intact and readable on one S-model express truck that was discovered in the 1980s with less than 100 miles recorded on the odometer.

Although a variety of cab styles were available, most S-model International trucks were delivered with enclosed cabs that appeared to be all steel, but were actually constructed by tacking steel panels onto a wooden framework. C-style cabs with their open sides were also popular and were similarly constructed of metal facings over a wooden framework. When an S-model truck has sat derelict for any period of time, usually both the outer metal and inner wooden framework have rotted, making cab restoration a major undertaking. To protect the driver against rain and snow, C-style cabs could be enclosed with side curtains. Enclosed cabs had glass roll-up or pull-up windows. Apart from the early Red Babies, the cab, fenders, and other sheet metal on an S-model truck is typically painted black lacquer.

While the headlights on the lighter duty S models are positioned in the usual location between the radiator shell and front fenders, the SD, SL, SF models, as well as the S-24 and S-26, placed the headlights on the cowl—a styling feature that easily distinguishes the larger trucks. International's heavier duty Three series, built at the new Fort Wayne, Indiana, plant also placed the headlights on the cowl. These larger trucks, designated model 33, 43, 63, and 103, shared basic styling with the S models but carried load ratings of up to 5 tons and used IH-manufactured engines, which shared crankshafts and blocks with tractor engines.

As was common practice at the time, International equipped its lighter duty S models with two-wheel, mechanically operated brakes, located at the rear wheels. Although the drums were large and the brakes of the internal-expanding type—which are more reliable in rain than the external contracting brake design used by some of the other manufacturers—there's not a lot of stopping power. Frank Heyman, who owns a Three-series International (which had similarly designed brakes, but at all four wheels) describes his truck's braking action like this:

"... going down hill with a load can be an experience if there is a curve or bridge at the bottom. You can easily run out of leg with the foot

Windshield wipers on early cars and trucks were hand-operated, a really distracting activity when driving in a rain or snow storm.

One wonders if any drivers actually looked at the markings on the clutch and brake pedals before shifting gears or bringing the truck to a stop.

brakes. That is where that LONG lever on the emergency brake (which operates on the outside of the rear drums) comes in handy. If you stand on the brakes and pull hard on the lever, you can get 'er shut down, but it takes some effort."

The quotation is from an interview published in *This Old Truck* magazine, December/January 1995.

On the lighter duty S models, the emergency brake works a little differently. For these trucks, the emergency brake shoes close against a drum mounted at the rear of the transmission. On both the S and Three series, the emergency brake lever is located just past the shift lever and not in an easy position to gain a lot of leverage for helping pull a moving truck to a stop.

Of course stopping isn't a concern until the truck is under way. Thanks to the electrical self-starter, coaxing life from the engine is a relatively simple process that begins by turning the ignition switch to IGN, retarding the spark by moving a lever located on the left side of the steering column underneath the steering wheel to the top position on its semi-circular track, then setting the throttle (the lever on the other side of the steering) about a quarter way down

its track, and pressing the starter pedal. It's an odd fact that the starter pedal can be found in two different locations on various model-S trucks. Sometimes the starter pedal is found on the floor directly beneath the driver's feet. Otherwise it is mounted on the firewall. The reason for change in location is probably that it's possible to step on the floor-mounted pedal while getting in and out of the vehicle—a potentially dangerous mistake. Moving the starter pedal to the firewall prevented this possibility.

The 3/4-ton Special Delivery, which had pioneered new markets for enclosed van-type trucks, was dropped as the series expanded for 1926. An all-new Special Delivery, now called the Series S Special Delivery, appeared in 1927. Like its predecessor, this model carried a 3/4-ton load rating, but the new delivery model had a more car-like appearance with a longer, lower hood, full length running boards, full crown fenders, drum headlights, and a nickel plated radiator shell. Both Special Delivery models used a Waukesha four-cylinder engine. Probably the Special Delivery's most significant achievement came in December 1927, when a specially fitted model set out on a reliability test across the Sahara Desert, a 6,618-mile trip orchestrated by International's export vice president for Africa, C. N. King. That the truck completed its grueling ordeal is as much a tribute to its driver and crew as to the ruggedness of the truck's design.

Another new model called the Six Speed Special, introduced mid-year 1927, proved an instant success. (Six Speed Special sales reached 50,000 units just three years.) The six speeds resulted from a two-speed rear end in combination with the three-speed transmission. International was the first manufacturer to offer such a combination in a light to medium duty truck and the concept was a "hit" from the day the first Six Speed Specials arrived

The Six Speed Special, introduced mid-year 1927, combined a two-speed rear end with the standard three-speed transmission. International was the first manufacturer to offer such a combination in a light to medium-duty truck, and the concept was a "hit" from the day the first Six Speed Specials arrived in dealer showrooms.

With the dual-speed rear axle, operators had both low-gear hauling power—for maneuvering in a field—plus higher road gearing for faster highway travel. The 1929 International Six Speed Special shown here is owned by Eugene Wentz.

in dealer showrooms. With the dual-speed rear axle, operators had both low-gear hauling power—for maneuvering in a field, pulling out of a gravel quarry, or traveling on deeply rutted country roads— plus higher road gearing for faster highway travel. With its full model lineup finally in place, International's truck sales reached an impressive total of 25,000 for all models, 3/4-ton to 5-ton, for 1927.

Load ranges for the Six Speed Special ran from 1 1/4 to 2 tons with wheelbase lengths from 117 inches to 160 inches. International was one of the first to offer trucks in a variety of sizes and body types within a fairly narrow load range to enable buyers to pick the truck best suited to their hauling needs. Besides stake and flatbeds, Six Speed Specials could be fitted with dump bodies, hoists, fuel tanks, fire apparatus, and other special equipment. International also sold Six Speed Specials in cab and chassis form to be fitted with bus and ambulance bodies provided by outside suppliers.

Although International trucks weren't the lowest priced on the market, they were competitive, particularly in relation to their sturdy construction and reputation for durability. In 1929, a

Four-wheel brakes, included on this truck, were a $25 option and well worth their cost in added stopping power.

Six Speed Special with a 124-inch wheelbase, fitted with enclosed cab and combination grain and stock body sold for $1,070. A bare cab and chassis for the same model could be purchased for $795. If purchased alone, a closed cab listed at $150. For fleet purchases, cabs could be ordered in prime for painting by the buyer at a $10 per truck savings. Four-wheel brakes were now an option, at $25 over base price. Other accessories and their costs included $5 for the nickel plated radiator shell, $25 for dual rear wheels, and $19 for a pair of Lovejoy shock absorbers. A speedometer added $25 to the truck's price.

International's S trucks and Six Speed Specials appealed to a variety of purposes from delivery work, either with enclosed or open bodies, to farm hauling (here combination grain and stock rack bodies were popular), to dump truck work (dump bodies made convenient off-loading of coal, which in those days was the most common heating fuel), to a variety of other tasks for which trucks used. Because of their large production, a fair number have survived, and today S-series models are the earliest IH trucks that can be said to be popular with collectors. These trucks are attractively styled and relatively speedy (for an early truck). But don't get the idea that an S truck, or even a Six Speed Special, is something to take on a long cruise. The combination of two-wheel brakes and truck gearing rule out extended highway travel. They make nice parade and show trucks, though. As noted earlier, if you are contemplating purchasing an S-series truck with an enclosed cab, carefully inspect the wooden body framework before making a purchase. Rotted cab wood will complicate the truck's restoration.

With the S models, International made itself a major player in the light- and medium-duty truck market. Models that follow would broaden and deepen that market.

The Six Speed Special's two-speed rear end had an auxiliary gear set ahead of the differential.

Right: Six Speed Special with the earlier S model's cab interior.

chapter four

1930-1933 A AND B SERIES:
International Unifies Its Truck Lineup

Although with its A- and B-series trucks International progressed in styling and amalgamated its truck lineup into an easily comprehensible sequence of models, today examples of these series are almost nonexistent. It's not because International suddenly fell on its face in the marketplace. Essentially, the dates of these model series tell the story. The A line appeared at the start of the Depression with the B models coming as the country's economy hit bottom. Even robust companies like International Harvester took a blow to the jugular as the nation's economy headed for the cellar. Then there was the price and competition. In the 1920s, buyers of International trucks wouldn't have been tempted to take a serious look at a Ford or Chevy. The gap in engineering, durability, and performance was too great. But with an A-series International Express truck listing at $890, and a Model-A Ford selling at roughly half that price, a would-be International buyer might take a harder look at the low-price competition. This isn't to suggest that a Model-A Ford pickup could stand up to a toe-to-toe comparison with an International: it couldn't. First, International's AW-1 "special delivery" carried a 3/4-ton rating. Ford's only light-duty truck model still used a car chassis and was fitted with such a small cargo box that some ingenuity was required to overburden the pickup's 1/2-ton rating with cargo other than rocks or pig iron. This disparity aside, there is

> Because of their scarcity and more than passing resemblance, many casual observers mistake an A/B-series International truck for a Model-A Ford truck of the 1930–1931 series. This beautifully restored 1934 Model-B International is owned by Matt Twilley.

more than a passing resemblance between an A-series International and a Model-A Ford truck of the 1930–1931 series.

When International introduced its A line in 1929, it did so with three new medium-duty models that were designed as replacements for the Three-series trucks. In keeping with the styling trends of the period, the new models featured taller radiators that placed the front of the hood nearly at cowl height. Of significance to sales people trying to help buyers select the right truck for their job, the new medium-duty A-line trucks used a simple numeric sequence: A-4, A-5, A-6 to represent increments in load rating. When the A line was complete (light-duty models would appear in 1930 and the heavy-duty models would be added in 1932), International succeeded in establishing an easily recognized scheme for differentiating its trucks by job classification. Beginning with the 3/4-ton A-1, the lineup now progressed to the A-2 and A-3 for the lighter duty range, to A-4 , A-5, and A-6 medium-duty models, and ended with the heavy-duty 5-ton rated A-7 and A-8. This number scheme surely benefited salesmen who no longer had to explain the difference between a Speed truck and a Six Speed Special. Since the same cab, grille, and front fender styling were used across the A line, International trucks now looked as if they belonged to the same family, regardless of size.

Prior to 1932, International had never—strictly speaking—built a pickup. As invented by Ford and Chevrolet, pickups were really cars fitted with a truck cab and small cargo box, not lighter duty general purpose trucks as International had been building. Rather than engineer its own pickup, International made a deal with Willys to supply that company's C-113 pickup, rebadged as an International D-1.

In 1932, International introduced rebadged Willys C-113 1/2-ton pickups and panels as its new D-1 models. The advertising for the new 1/2-ton models was somewhat deceptive as the prominently stated $360 price was for a bare chassis—and who, apart from a station wagon builder, would buy just a chassis?

Light-duty A models joined the A line in mid-1930 with the 3/4-ton rated AW-1 Special Delivery. This truck had a wheelbase of 136 inches and continued many of the mechanical features of the 1920s Speed trucks, including the Waukesha L-4 engine. The AW-1 could be purchased as a cab and chassis (that's the way it's shown on the cover of the Special Delivery Instruction Book) on which the owner could mount any variety of bodies, canopy delivery, screenside express, panel truck, and sedan delivery bodies being the more popular choices. Since one of the AW-1's configurations was as an Express, buyers could order their truck with a wooden express box and rear fenders. The longer wheelbase and overall heavier duty construction, including beefy rear load springs, placed the AW-1 more in the cargo carrying category of a Ford AA Express than a Model-A Ford pickup. Like the early Ford AA models, the International AW-1 used single rear wheels, rather than duals, though they were 20-inch and of rugged steel spoke construction.

Next up the line, International marketed an AW-2, which was really an updated version of the popular Six Speed Special. This truck shared the AW-1's 173-cubic inch Waukesha engine and 136-inch wheelbase, but was fitted with a two-speed rear axle as standard equipment. Buyers considered the AW-2 more of a medium-duty model, and usually fitted their trucks with a grain body or stake bed.

Surely one of the most appreciated features of International's A-series light-duty trucks was the new fully enclosed cab, which added 2 inches in length to accommodate lanky drivers and featured a smart "cadet visor" over the windshield to shield the driver's eyes from a low evening or morning sun. The "cadet" part of the visor's description refers to the short "bill" on the hats of military cadets. Windshield wipers were now listed as standard equipment—anyone who has ever driven a vehicle with inoperable windshield wipers can appreciate the importance of this seemingly insignificant feature.

For the A series International's standard cab color was a gray-green lacquer, with fenders and splash aprons painted black. Like most automotive body construction of the period, the cab on A-line trucks consisted of stamped sheets of metal tacked to a wooden frame. Although this construction gave the appearance of an all-metal body, in fact the metal exterior was only "skin" deep, the structural substance of the cab being wood. Since this wooden framework is highly susceptible to rot, the few A-series International trucks that have survived usually present the challenge of fabricating

Beginning with the A-4 models, all medium-and heavy-duty A-series trucks used heavy-duty, overhead valve six-cylinder engines designed and built by International.

new wood on which to hang the cab sheet metal—a task that requires the talents and tools of a skilled woodworker.

As International fleshed out the A series with new models, the new trucks often appeared in competition with those already in production. For example, in 1931 two new light-duty models, the A-1 and A-2, lined up beside the AW-1 and AW-2. Both the A-1 and AW-1 carried the same 3/4-ton rating, but the A-1 had a larger 186-cubic inch Waukesha XAH four cylinder engine, still of L-head design. Upgrades to the engine included pressure oiling, rubber cushioned rear engine mounts, and a water pump as standard equipment. The A-1 also featured a four-speed transmission, more suitable for truck use. In a nutshell, the A-1 represented an upscale version of the AW-1. On the A-2 buyers could specify a longer 160-inch wheelbase. This truck also had the four-speed transmission, but not the AW-2's two-speed rear axle. To purchase a six-speed truck from International, the buyer had to specify the new B-2 model, which revived the name Six Speed Special. An interesting feature of this truck, the dual-speed rear axle could be engaged in reverse—giving two speeds in that direction as well.

For truck buyers shopping in the light-duty range, but needing more hauling power,

International offered the A-3, which used a Lycoming six-cylinder engine with a 223-cubic inch displacement. The smart salesman would point out to a potential A-3 buyer the Lycoming engine's advantages, which were more than just larger size. The Lycoming possessed many advanced engineering features, including aluminum alloy pistons, insert-type main bearings, and force feed lubrication, that added up to greater durability—as well as more power. Since the A-1, A-2, and A-3 all shared the same wheelbase, International's engineers made the longer six-cylinder engine fit by giving the A-3s a longer hood.

Beginning with the A-4 models, all medium- and heavy-duty A-series trucks now used heavy-duty, overhead valve six-cylinder engines designed and built by International. Over the next several years, International would design a new, lighter weight overhead valve engine for its medium-duty models and then purchase the patents and tooling for another engine used in the light duty trucks. By the end of the 1930s, engines in all its truck models would be built by International.

As America's economic Depression worsened, International tried a variety of methods to spark sales and save jobs. As one incentive, International offered to pay employees who helped sell a new

One of the most appreciated features of International's A- and B-series trucks was the fully-enclosed cab, which was not only wider to accommodate three men, but also added two-inches in length for longer-legged drivers and featured a smart "cadet visor" over the windshield to shield the driver's eyes from a low evening or morning sun.

Despite the bleak economic climate, International continued to refine and introduce new products. Just a few years prior to the A line's introduction, International had built elaborate test facilities at Springfield, Ohio, and a technical research facility at the Fort Wayne plant in Indiana. Now, to more easily check out prototypes and shake down new production models, the company built another test track near Fort Wayne. The investment in testing and research paid off by assuring customers that International trucks were built to the highest standards.

Have your heart set on finding a light-duty B-model International? If it's the early 1930s B series you're talking about, you can call off the search. There's no such vehicle. International did build B-3 and B-4 models in its medium-duty line, the difference with their A-line counterparts being mainly mechanical. As one point of distinction, these so-called B models appear to be the first IH trucks with a downdraft carburetor. Other improvements over earlier models include a fuel pump, as opposed to the sometimes unreliable vacuum fuel delivery system, and relocating the water pump to the front of the engine.

By 1933 International had completed the switch from solid rubber to pneumatic tires on all its trucks, even the heavy-duty models. On the light-duty models, balloon tires were now used, giving a more comfortable ride. The cast spoke wheels installed on all early 1930 International trucks, from heavy-duty down to the light-duty models, could almost be considered an IH trademark.

International Fields a Pickup

Prior to 1932, International had never—strictly speaking—built a pickup. Its light-duty S-model and A-line trucks with their wooden pickup-like bodies were labeled as Express Trucks. Pickups, as invented by Ford and Chevrolet, were really cars fitted with a truck cab and small cargo box. Though hardly trucks in the sense of being able to carry a respectable load, the light-duty pickups were strong sellers, popular with farmers for whom they were often the family's only vehicle, and with a variety of businesses that needed an economical means of transporting small cargo. Despite its sales potential, the pickup didn't fit into International's manufacturing scheme. But how about selling someone else's pickup under the International nameplate? What would probably have been unthinkable in good economic times made practical sense at the depths of the Depression. So when International approached Willys about re-badging that company's C-113 pickup as the D-1

truck a bonus of $5 to $25, the size of the truck determining the amount of the bonus. International also sought sales in foreign markets, particularly in South America, and opened a plant in England. Since Europe was also experiencing economic depression, the English venture was short-lived.

International, the Toledo, Ohio, based manufacturer quickly signed the deal.

When the Willys name is remembered today, it's usually for that world-famous automotive product, the Jeep. But at the time International and Willys signed their pickup deal, the Jeep wasn't even a dream in anybody's mind and Willys best-known products were luxury cars powered by almost dead-silent sleeve-valve engines. Since the Depression had all but shut down the luxury car market, Willys had quickly developed the 1/2-ton pickup and a companion panel delivery, both of which it introduced in 1931. Called the C-113, the light trucks took their name from their 113-inch wheelbase. Powering the new trucks was a freshly designed 193-cubic inch six-cylinder engine that incorporated such important longevity features as replaceable insert bearings and pressure-feed oiling to all main and connecting rod bearings, the camshaft, and timing chain. Reflecting its modern design, this new six had higher compression and produced its power at a higher rpm than earlier engines. For its D-1 pickup, International specified that this engine's displacement be increased to 213 cubic inches, thereby adding 5 horsepower. Under International badges the pickup's engine developed 70 horsepower. Eventually, International would purchase manufacturing rights to the C-113 engine from Willys, and under the name Green Diamond this well-engineered engine would gain a reputation for reliability and dependability in International trucks through the K and KB series of the 1940s.

International's light-duty D-1 trucks appeared at dealers in January 1933. Although the typical configuration was as a pickup or panel truck, the D-1 could be purchased as a bare chassis on which a buyer mounted the body of his choice—such as a woody station wagon. Although no D-1 woody wagons are known to exist, one could be authentically replicated. The bare chassis sold for only $360, a fact International displayed prominently in its ads. International even went so far as to boast that a comparable light truck chassis could not be purchased for under $600.

Having used the D-1 designation on its 1933 light-duty line, there came a question what to call the light-duty models when International introduced its D line in 1937. As we shall see later in this book, potential confusion was eliminated by labeling the 1/2-ton D-series truck model the D-2.

Probably the most noticeable styling feature of both the D-1 pickup and the panel is the flared out opening around the windshield, which gives the front of the vehicle a sort of tunneled-in appearance. To give a family resemblance with

Steel wheels and semielliptic front springs gave International's medium-duty trucks an edge on the competition. The headlights on this truck are nonstandard.

the A-line trucks, International reworked the D-1's radiator and hood, which on the Willys version have a more car-like appearance.

On D-1 models, the instrument cluster consisted of individually shaped gauges nested in a uniquely styled dash with a rectangular, tunneled portion in the center. The spark, throttle, choke, and heat control knobs reside in the dash, while the starter, light, and horn controls are placed in an odd position (used uniquely by Willys) on the top of the steering column. The rest of the controls can be found in their usual 1930s location, except the emergency brake lever, which is mounted on the left side of the cab.

Besides contributing its engine to later International light-duty models, the D-1 initiated a design feature in which the rear springs mount directly under the frame rails. (For its 3/4-ton Special Delivery and heavier models, International mounted the rear springs "outrigger" from the frame.) On the C-113/D-1 and later IH light duty trucks, the frame channel spread apart toward the rear of the chassis for better load distribution and stability.

As with the A-line trucks, the light-duty D-1 models were painted gray green, unless the customer ordered a special color. Optional equipment included a chrome-plated rear bumper, pedestal-mounted side view mirror (to perch on top of the side-mounted tire), dual tail lights, a spotlight, and cowl lamps.

To join the ranks of the mainstream truck builders, International needed a pickup. Though its venture with Willys put it on track, International's next step was to make its pickup "home grown."

chapter five

C- AND D-SERIES TRUCKS:
Automotive Styling Comes to International's Truck Line

If you took the front half of a C-series International pickup, cut off the back of the cab, and extended the body so that it made a two-passenger coupe, or even a sedan, you'd have one swell-looking car. For many automotive historians, the 1930s represent a high-water mark of automotive and light-duty truck styling. International's C-series pickups wear several prized styling features of the era, including the clam-shell front fenders, V'd grille, and wire-spoke wheels.

Yet in a truck, function counts as much as appearance, and in this area, too, the C series stands tall. To make getting into and out of the cab easier, designers widened the doors. To keep the cab from feeling like a furnace on hot summer days, a ventilator on the cowl and swing-out windshield could be opened to duct outside air into the driving compartment. For easy viewing and to monitor vital engine functions, instruments were now grouped in two circular gauge clusters positioned toward the center of the dash.

With the C series, International greatly expanded its truck line, which now included 33 different variations of 15 basic models. On the light-duty end, International now built its own 1/2-ton pickup, which it labeled appropriately the C-1. Although all-new in appearance, the C-1 shared the 113-inch wheelbase and L-6 engine of its Willys-built D-1 predecessor. The engine, however, was now an International product, see-

> Although later International pickups were often painted red, green seems to be a favorite color on D-series trucks. George Schroyer owns this handsome 1939 D-2 pickup.

ing that IH had purchased patents and tooling. For those needing a little larger light-duty truck, International offered the C-10, a 3/4-ton model on a 133-inch wheelbase, powered by a 186-cubic inch four-cylinder Waukesha XAH engine and fitted with a four-speed transmission. At the top of the light duty-range the C-20 carried a load rating of 1 to 1 1/2-ton, depending on wheelbase (133-inch or 157-inch) and shared the C-10's Waukesha engine. The C-series medium-duty line extended from the C-30, a 1 1/2-ton-rated model available on either a 133-inch or 157-inch wheelbase (sales brochures for 1936 also list a 172-inch wheelbase C-30 model; to the C-35 2-ton truck with International's overhead valve 223 motor. At the heavy-duty end, came the C-40, C-50, C-55, C60. For the first time International offered a Cab Over Engine model, designated the C-300. The C-30 was the company's biggest seller, but the light-duty C-1 pickup is most popular today with restorers. Since the light-duty chassis could also be used as a platform for special bodies like woody station wagons, it's even possible to build a restored International C-series truck with the highly desirable woody wagon body.

In 1936, the last year of the C series, IH added more new models—presumably to fill perceived market gaps. The C-5, a 1/2-ton truck with a four-cylinder Waukesha engine, seems to have been aimed at light-duty truck buyers looking for

As Kenneth Rabeneck, who owns this beautiful 1936 C-1 pickup, discovered, the biggest challenge for those restoring a C-series International truck is the lack of replacement parts. Unlike Fords and Chevrolets, for which reproduction parts are available even for 1930s models, with International, the only options are new or used original parts. Rabeneck joined truck clubs to get in touch with other collectors, advertised in *Hemmings*, went to shows, and talked to people everywhere. "Talking to people, that's what really helped," Rabeneck says. Rather than repair the rusty bed, a friend who works with sheet metal made a new one. Only the tailgate and brackets are original. The windshield and rear window frames were another big problem. Rabeneck bought a 1935 C-30 just for the frames. The bumper and hubcaps were beaten up, but here replacements weren't available, and after four and a half years of looking, Rabeneck gave up and repaired what he had. The work was worth it, and today Rabeneck's truck is a showpiece. *Courtesy of* This Old Truck *magazine*

optimum fuel economy. Although gasoline was cheap in the 1930s, these were very bleak economic times and many truck owners were trying to shave operating expenses as closely as possible. Oddly, since it was equipped with a less powerful engine, the C-5 could be specified with a longer 125-inch wheelbase. (Both the C-1 and C-5 came standard with a 113-inch wheelbase, and a longer 125-inch C-1 was now also available.) Despite its low sales, International management believed the C-5 filled an important segment of its truck line-up and continued to build a comparable truck in the soon to be forthcoming D series.

The basic light-duty offering was a so-called cowl and chassis, basically a bare-bones truck to which the buyer added some sort of aftermarket

With commercial vehicles, it was common for the manufacturer to mount the spare in the passenger side fender: reason, the tire partially obstructed the opening angle of the door, something an occasional passenger could put up with better than the driver. *Courtesy of* This Old Truck *magazine*

International built the Metro as a delivery truck for a variety of retail and service businesses. In this case, the truck's operator is an International dealership.

cargo body. Among the available body configurations none was more fashionable than the woody station wagon mentioned earlier. Quite a large number of C-1 and C-5 models were fitted out as telephone company trucks. On these a square utility body replaced the pickup box and brackets from the front and rear fenders held the telephone lineman's ladder. Enough of this model survive that C-series telephone lineman's trucks can occasionally be seen at antique truck shows. Extra cost accessories for the C-1 or C-5 included a rear bumper, side-mounted tire, a pedestal mirror for the sidemount, bumper guards, dual windshield wipers, dual tail lights, and beauty (trim) rings for the wheels.

New models at the other end of the light-duty range consisted of the C-12 and C-15, longer wheelbase entries in the 3/4 to 1-ton class that used the C-1's 213 L6 engine. Oddly, the C-15, the heavier duty of the two, had a three-speed transmission,

In the 1960s, International introduced this restyled Metro, designated AM 150, with a more modern looking squared-off body. This 1961 Metro AM 150 model is owned by George Mitchell.

Since International sold its trucks worldwide, it should be no surprise to see this C-series International flatbed truck parked at the completion of the historic "London to Brighton" run, held annually in England. This British International wears a custom body builder's cab as well as the unusual flatbed body. *Dwight Giles*

International sold its light duty C-1 in cab and chassis form so the buyer could mount a special-purpose cargo body, such as the utility box fitted to this telephone lineman's truck, originally purchased and outfitted by Pennsylvania Bell.

while the C-12 was fitted with a four-speed. Normally the heavier load-rated truck would be expected to have the wider gearing range.

The two-speed rear axle that had made the earlier Six Speed Specials such popular trucks were now available on the C-30 and C-35, and when so equipped, these models were designated CS-30 and CS-35 (the S referring to the two-speed rear axle). Note that with the C series, the two-speed rear axle was no longer available on 1-ton trucks, but only on 1 1/2-ton and larger models. Besides the two-speed rear axle, International's medium-duty trucks could be fitted with auxiliary rear springs and a power takeoff mounted on the transmission. While most trucks sold in this load range carried stake bodies, IH sales literature shows a panel body on their medium duty chassis.

International continued to build its light duty trucks at Springfield, Ohio, and heavy-duty models at Ft. Wayne, Indiana. Gradually improving economic conditions and the more appealing styling made the C series a strong seller, and by the end of 1936, the Springfield plant alone had built 80,000 C-line trucks. Thanks to the C line's success, International was once again in third place among U.S. truck manufacturers.

Aside from the new models, some rather subtle as well as significant changes occurred through the C series' three-year run. As a minor change, in 1935 C-1 trucks were fitted with steel-disk wheels as standard equipment, the more attractive steel-spoke wheels becoming an extra-cost accessory. The more substantial changes occurred in 1936, when all International trucks were fitted with four-wheel hydraulic brakes. The previous braking mechanism had been mechanical, and although mechanical brakes are reliable, they don't give the stopping power of hydraulics. Another important change, during the 1936 model run, cab door construction was changed to all-metal from the earlier method of attaching inner and outer sheet metal to a wooden framework. Unlike metal, which can be repaired by welding, wooden framed construction requires a cabinet maker's skills and tools and is very difficult to restore. The cabs of International's C-series trucks still contained some wood, most notably the floor boards. Since these wooden pieces help maintain the shape of the lower floor, if they are rotted, they must be carefully duplicated to original measurements.

The biggest challenge for those restoring a C-series International truck is the lack of replacement parts. Unlike Fords and Chevrolets, where reproduction parts are available even for 1930s models, with International the only options are original parts, new or used. Mechanical parts for the C-1's 213 cubic inch six-cylinder engine are another story, however. Since this engine was used in light-duty International trucks into the late 1940s, many parts can be ordered "next day delivery" from local auto parts stores.

The grain box on this D-2 International gives the impression that it is larger than a 1/2-ton model. The D-2 designation itself leads some truck fanciers to think they're looking at a heavier duty 3/4-ton truck. The confusion results from International's having called the Willys-built pickup that sold alongside the A line in 1933 and 1934 a D-1 model. Thus the 1/2-ton D model became the D-2. *Courtesy of* This Old Truck *magazine*

The 1/2-ton pickup, which International originally bought from Willys, turned out to be a winner. Part of the reason may have been buyer preference for the C-1's more powerful six-cylinder engine over the four cylinder Waukesha engines used in the larger capacity but less nimble C-10. International would rectify this in its upper end of its light-duty offerings with its D-series line, introduced in the spring of 1937. Until that date, the C-series trucks continued to attract buyers through their built-in sales appeal.

1937–1940 D Series

Art deco, a form of art and architectural design best recognized for its emphasis on horizontal and vertical lines, became a major styling influence on automotive design of the late 1930s. One of the best examples is the 810-812 "coffin nose" Cord with "ribs" that wrap around the nose of the car and extend back along the sides of the hood in a a clear reflection of the art deco motif. It's expected that car styling will mirror dominant art forms, but trucks are usually just considered utility vehicles designed to do a job. For those who see trucks as

strictly functional, the D-series International presents a different view. Sure, International's D-series trucks are utilitarian, designed for work, but they also capture that fleet, streamlined art deco image, impressed through the grille lines that, like those of the Cord 810/812, sweep back along the sides of the hood.

It's no accident that the D series has such distinctive styling. Like the process used to execute a new car design, the D's cab and frontal shape took form first as concept sketches, the most promising of which were then modeled in clay. From these life-like three-dimensional renderings management selected designs for further refinement. Modern-looking as the production D-line trucks were, one of the styling exercises projected an even more striking design with full-fender skirts covering both the front and rear wheels and trim streaks that wrapped across the front of the hood above the grille and extended back across the hood and doors. The spare tire in this rendering was enclosed in a cover like those used on cars of the day and the headlights were set into the fenders to give a smooth frontal look. Although

Mark Romano literally saved this 1938 D-2 from the crusher. The dry goods display that accompanies the truck was assembled one item at a time. The Jumbo Oats box was in his garage being used as a toy box when Mark put it in the D-2. A neighbor saw the box and donated an old ice cream can to keep it company. Mark bought some seed bags and when his mother saw them she added a couple more. His wife Pam found the milk can at a flea market and a nail keg at an antique shop. "I never know what is going to show up in the back of my truck," Romano says. *Courtesy of* This Old Truck *magazine*

these features never saw production, elements that reached production can also be seen in this sketch, including the D line's short running boards, high windshield "eye brows," and rounded side door windows.

Once the truck's styling had been finalized and prototypes built, these preproduction trucks were put through rigorous testing, both on the paved highway and rough torture roads at International's new proving grounds located near the Fort Wayne plant. When the trucks broke down or were torn apart, the causes were identified and engineering changes made to the production models. When Commodore Attilio Gatti selected D-series station wagons for an African expedition that traveled 66,000 miles through largely uncharted regions of what today is called the country of Zaire, International publicized both the adventure of the expedition and the trucks' repair cost, which totaled only $68. Clearly the rigorous preproduction testing process had paid off.

International's D-series trucks, which first appeared in March 1937, are easily identified by their rounded grille that merges at the top with chrome bars and louvers that extend back along the sides of the hood. The V'd two-piece windshield gave better visibility than the former flat windshields, and although not large by modern standards, the rear window was wider and deeper than previously and was oval shaped to harmonize with the cab's rounded styling. The high-crowned, pontoon style front fenders copied the fender design of expensive, high-powered cars like certain Duesenbergs and the British LG-45 Lagonda Rapide, which raced at LeMans, but somehow the fenders also looked right on International's fleet D-series trucks.

While most of the D line's styling features are bold enough to stand out, even on the first encounter with a truck from this series, some of the changes from earlier models are more subtle and take closer observation to recognize. For example, on pickups and panels, the running boards now

While most of the D line's styling features are bold enough to stand out, even on the first encounter with a truck from this series, some of the changes from earlier D models are more subtle and take closer observation to recognize. For example, on pickups and panels the running boards now stopped at the rear of the door for a functional and more modern look.

stopped at the rear of the door, for a functional and more modern look. On C line and earlier International light-duty trucks, the running boards ran full length between the front to back fenders. To blend the running boards into the body, the cab now extended below the door, a space filled on earlier models by sheet metal pieces called "splash aprons." The cargo box on pickup models now had reinforcing ribs on the sides for greater strength

and the stake pockets were now built into the box sides, rather than being tack-welded on, as had formerly been the case.

The D series brought many other important changes besides styling that were more than "skin deep." Cabs were now of all-steel construction for greater strength and durability. Deeper door windows gave more glass area and the windows now had rounded corners to match the contours of the

With the D series came a new nameplate with more purposeful looking lettering that would be used into the mid-1950s.

cab. A wider cab, now measuring 60 inches across, enabled three men to sit abreast in moderate comfort. The rectangular-shaped gauge cluster, which was placed squarely in front of the driver, picked up the Art Deco styling theme through a ribbed bezel. Grouping the gauges for water temperature, generator charging rate, oil pressure, and fuel level around a square central speedometer enabled the operator to monitor the truck's speed and mechanical vital signs in a glance. If installed, a radio was mounted in the center of the dash, under the windshield crank handle.

It's easy to see the D-2 designation on a 1/2-ton model in this series and think you're looking at a heavier duty 3/4-ton truck. But remember there had already been a D-1, the Willys-built pickup that International sold alongside the A line in 1933 and 1934. So to avoid confusion, the 1/2-ton D model is designated the D-2. Initially, the D-2 chassis was available only on a 113-inch wheelbase, the same as its C-1 predecessor. However, the overall length of a 113-inch wheelbase D-2 pickup measures about four inches longer than a C-1. The additional length resulted from International's moving the engine and cab ahead on the chassis to create a better weight balance.

Later in the series, in 1939, two 1/2-ton wheelbases, 113 inches and 125 inches, were made available. Now a pickup could be ordered with either a short 6 1/2-foot box or long 7 1/2-foot box. Besides the pickups, D-2 body styles included stake beds, panel deliveries, canopy express, and woody station wagons, and the 1/2-ton Metro. Modified panel trucks used as ambulances and mail trucks completed the D-series light-duty truck roster. Extra-cost equipment

International Offers a Cabover

With the growth in long-distance trucking, there also came an increase in short haul, inner city trucking. The narrow streets and alleys in which this inner city commerce moved called for a new truck design that allowed greater maneuverability in tight spaces. International's engineers recognized that the only practical way to increase a truck's maneuverability was by decreasing its overall length. The question was how to cut back on the truck's length without losing cargo area. The answer came in reducing the truck's frontal area. The result was an all-new truck style that tucked the engine underneath the driving compartment, eliminating the long "nose" or hood area. The new style, called the "forward control" or "cabover engine" first appeared in 1935 in the C series, under the designation C300.

The first cabover models experienced low sales due to engine noise and heat, so the design was improved, but left visually unchanged for the D series, the new designation being the D300. With a flat front, large windshield area, and high seating position, the cabover truck gave the driver excellent visibility The cab doors hinged in the normal (forward) location, which enabled the driver to open the door and look around the side of the truck to check for clearance and obstacles when backing up to loading docks or into alleys. Since cabover trucks lacked running boards, the driver climbed into the cab by mounting steps attached to the front fender.

In the 1960s and later the cabover design would come to dominate in International's distance hauling semitractor/trailer rigs for much the same reason as the C300/D300 models, maximum load length, excellent driver visibility, and greater maneuverability in tight spaces.

International's D-series trucks show the influence of art deco design, particularly in the grille with its rows of slim horizontal lines.

Many owners of vintage pickups wonder why the lock cylinder is found only on the passenger door. The reason goes like this: In cities, trucks were used for deliveries and it was thought that the driver might be struck by a passing vehicle if he got out of the cab on the left side. Putting the door lock on the right side caused the driver to lock his door by the inside handle, then slide across the seat and exit the truck onto the sidewalk on the right.

included a deluxe cab with a slide-open rear window and arm rests, low-speed cut-in generators for city delivery use, an engine oil filter, and a hot water heater with defroster.

Because of the popularity of the D-2 models, even many International enthusiasts are not aware that in the D series, International continued to build two 1/2-ton models: the six-cylinder powered D-2 and a four-cylinder engined D-5. Most of the body offerings for the D-2 were also available on the D-5, except the station wagon. The reason for continuing a four-cylinder 1/2-ton line was for operating economy.

At the upper end of the light-duty class, International again offered a 3/4-ton model, designated the D-15, which also used the 213 six. This truck was also available in two chassis lengths on 113-inch and 130-inch wheelbases. The D-15 body offerings included an express, stake, canopy, panel, and station wagon.

Due to the steel companies being able to supply sheet steel in wider dimensions, the D-series panel trucks now had an all-steel roof. On D-2 and D-5 1/2-ton panel trucks, the interior cargo area measured a spacious 94 3/8 inches front to rear. Long wheel-base D-15 panel models had an uninterrupted 109 3/8 inches of cargo space. The flooring in the cargo area was of sturdy ship-lapped lumber. In standard form, the panel trucks were fitted with a single adjustable seat, rearview mirror, electric windshield wipers, safety glass, a dome light, combination stop and taillight, tool box, cowl vent, spare wheel, and cover. On panel trucks optional equipment included an extra seat, dual windshield wipers, chromed windshield frame, rear bumper, spare tire, and lock.

The woody station wagon is probably the most attractive and desirable of all body types offered in the D line. International supplied the chassis, but did not build the woody body. When a customer wanted a D-series station wagon he purchased a D-2 or D-15 chassis and specified whether he wanted International to install a wooden station wagon body built by Cantrell, Hercules, or Moller. Of the three, the Moller body was the most deluxe. For this Hagerstown, Maryland, company, building woody station wagon bodies was a sideline to its primary business, constructing pipe organs. During the Depression several companies that had formerly built pianos and organs survived a declining market for musical instruments by putting their craftsmen to work on other products, such as boats, or, in Moller's case, woody station wagons. The pipe organ heritage shows, and Moller bodies are exceptionally well crafted. Besides a plate with the manufacturer's name (which may or may not still be attached) a Moller body is easily distinguished by roll-up side windows. On a woody body built by Cantrell or Hercules , sliding side windows were used.

Station wagons could be ordered on either the 1/2-ton 113 or 3/4-ton 130-inch chassis. On the shorter chassis, the woody body was designed to carry eight passengers, while the longer chassis woody would carry twelve. Usually the longer wheelbase woody station wagons were used as small busses by private day

The Metro—
Built Small on the Outside, but
Big on the Inside

Probably no one at IH realized that the Metro delivery truck, introduced in 1939, would remain in production basically unchanged through 1964. So good was the Metro's original design that it lasted a full quarter-century. It was not the all-time production longevity record (the VW Beetle had a longer run, counting its Mexican and South American versions) but a close runner-up.

International built the Metro as a delivery truck for stores, wholesalers, bakeries, laundries, dry cleaners, dairies, florists, grocers, and any other business that needed a stylish vehicle that could haul bulky loads and maneuver easily in city traffic. To meet these requirements, the Metro was made as compact as possible on the outside, but as roomy as possible on the inside, with care also given to making the vehicles easy as possible to load, unload, and drive.

The original Metro appeared in the D series and came in two sizes, the 102-inch wheelbase D-2-M, which had an overall length of 7 feet 9 inches, and the 113-inch wheelbase D-15-M, which measured 9 feet 6 inches in overall length. International built only the Metro chassis; bodies came from Metropolitan Body Co. in Bridgeport, Connecticut. Metros had an all-metal body with sliding front doors. A one-piece flexible steel rear door rolled upward into the roof and was counterbalanced so that it would stay at the height it was opened. Referred to in company advertising as the "Metro Magic" rear door, its design enabled drivers to back the van tight against a delivery dock and still open the truck's loading door. For businesses requiring a wide loading space for bulky items, Metros could be fitted with double rear doors on special order. To keep the van's interior warm in the winter and cool in the summer, the body maker placed glass-wool insulation in the roof and allowed a dead-air space between the outer and inner body panels.

The Metro design showed that much attention had been paid to the driver's convenience and comfort. Controls were placed within easy reach: the gearshift lever being located on the steering column and the hand brake handle at the driver's left. Flat panels on top of the engine cover made a convenient place to lay parcels for the next delivery. The wide windshield gave the driver excellent forward visibility, while narrow side pillars and front quarter windows offered a nearly 180-degree field of view from inside the truck.

The Metro's small exterior is deceiving. On short wheelbase models, the cargo area measures 93 inches long by 70 inches wide and 68 inches high, for a total of 225 cubic feet of cargo capacity.

Initially, International supplied the Metro with a black chassis and body in prime, allowing the buyer to apply his own color scheme. Chromed grille, lamp rims, hub caps, and bumpers gave all Metros a deluxe look. Standard equipment included front and rear bumpers, a spare wheel and carrier, a dome light, adjustable driver's seat, windshield wiper, left hand rear view mirror, tool box, package compartment, front and rear door locks, and the Metro Magic rear door. Options included a right-hand rear view mirror, dual windshield wipers, an extra dome light, double rear doors, a partition with a sliding door behind the driver's compartment, and squared rear wheelwell housings. The last option helped with stacking loose items, but was not needed when a Metro was used, for example, as a portable workshop for a plumbing business.

With few and relatively minor changes, the Metro moved from the D to the K and KB series and on to the L, R, and S lines. Finally designated the AM-150 and 160, the Metro remained in production until 1964. In the K series, buyers could purchase their Metro factory painted. Having a short wheelbase Metro factory painted cost the buyer $43, while painting a long wheelbase Metro added $52 to the base invoice. In 1945, dual side-hinged rear doors became standard and the Metro Magic rear door was made an option. A single 60-inch side-hinged rear door could also be specified as an extra cost option. Rear fender skirts were eliminated in the KB series and the shape of the headlight rims was changed from oval to round. In the R line the Metro was joined by the Metroette, a traditional engine-forward delivery, while Metro also underwent a changes. The longer wheelbase version was stretched slightly to 115 inches and a new body with squared-off rear corners and double rear doors joined the familiar style Metro. In 1954 an automatic "MetroMatic" transmission became standard equipment. In the passage of time the Metro grille was revised for more space between the horizontal slats, parking lights were added and placed below the headlights, the IH insignia was added to the center of the grille, the front bumper was painted instead of chromed, and the delivery received the light-duty truck line's improved engines.

Although a success by delivery truck standards, Metro production never approached the sales volume of International's pickup trucks so today a Metro makes a highly unusual, and in that sense desirable, collector vehicle.

The D series brought many important changes besides styling. Cabs were now of all-steel construction for greater strength and durability; the panel models now had an all-steel roof; and all light-duty models were offered with a floor-shift, synchromesh three-speed transmission.

schools, camps, lodges, or resort hotels. For the short wheelbase station wagon, seating consisted of a fixed front bench seat, center folding seats, and a rear bench seat. Passengers sitting in the center or rear seats entered through a door on the passenger side.

International used just one color on its station wagons, which were painted tan with matching tan upholstery and tops. Due to the weight of the wooden body, the 213 engine worked rather hard just moving an empty vehicle, which weighed over 2 tons. As a result, most woody wagons were fitted with the optional four-speed transmission.

In the sales department, International's D-series trucks were a big hit. Production for 1937 topped 100,000, setting an all-time sales record that put International in third place among

American truck builders. Although collectors today favor the light-duty models, buyers in 1937 preferred the 1 1/2-ton models. But the light duties set sales records too. Between 1937 and 1940, D-2 production passed 80,000 units. Profits generated by the strong truck sales enabled International to build a new engine plant, which the company decided to locate in Indianapolis, Indiana, a city halfway between International's Springfield, Ohio, light-duty truck plant and its Fort Wayne, Indiana, heavy truck assembly plant. With construction work proceeding at full pace, the new engine facility opened in mid-1939.

For the D line, the Willys-derived 213-cubic inch six-cylinder engine, which appears under the hood in the D-2 and D-15 light-duty models, saw several design improvements. These changes included full-length water jackets, a different intake manifold casting, and a more efficient combustion chamber design. Thus upgraded, the mainstay engine of International's light-duty fleet produced 78 horsepower at 3,400 rpm. In contrast, the 17-cubic inch four-cylinder economy engine offered in the D-5 line delivered only 46 horsepower.

International fitted all D-series light-duty models with a floor-shift synchromesh three-speed transmission as standard equipment. A four-speed transmission could be specified at extra cost. Since the four-speed transmission featured straight-cut gears (International wouldn't offer a four-speed transmission with synchromesh until the 1950s on the L series), operators of four-speed D-series trucks had to develop the knack for double-clutching—a technique for matching the engine revolutions to the truck's speed—to make silent shifts.

In 1940, along with the rest of the industry, International's D-line trucks received sealed beam headlights. (Noticing the sealed beam lights is the quickest way to recognize a 1940 model.) Also in 1940, a new D-2H model (a slightly beefed-up D-2 truck on the 125-inch wheelbase) was introduced for pickup buyers wanting greater load capacity than the standard 1/2-ton. This model was continued in the K line as the K-2. For 1940, the D-15 also could be ordered in two load ranges, the 3/4-ton mentioned previously and a D-15H with a 1-ton rating. Both D-15 models used the longer 130-inch wheelbase. Although the restyled K line replaced the D series in late 1940, the D cab remained in service in the larger K-series trucks (K-6 and up) with very minor changes.

chapter six

1940-1949 K AND KB SERIES:
A Truck to Fit Every Job

With 42 models and 142 different wheelbase lengths, the K line represented the greatest range of truck models and load ratings in International's history. Load ratings ranged from 1/2-ton to 90,000 pounds. The company's ads said it well: buyers could now find an International truck ". . . to fit every job like a glove." In the light-duty range, the lineup differed little from the D series—which already included practically every desired body type from pickup or platform/stake to panel truck, canopy express, station wagon, or a bare cab/chassis on which customers could mount any number of special purpose bodies to suit a variety of purposes, such as towing truck booms. Since there was now no obstacle to designating the 1/2-ton model as a K-1, the number scheme now progressed logically to K-2 for 3/4-ton; and K-3 for the 1-ton, etc. up to the K-6, 7, and 8 heavy-duty models. In the light-duty range, the K-1 and K-2 models mostly shared the same mechanical and chassis components, as is typical in these load ranges even today, while the K-3 had a beefier construction.

Keeping pace with then-current styling trends, the headlights were placed in the fenders for an integrated frontal look. The grille, which retained a traditional vertical profile, was now capped by a long hood that opened alligator-style. All models, including pickups and panels, now used short running boards—a first step toward the elimination of a one-time convenience

> The panel truck body featured welded-steel construction with plywood flooring. These no-frills vehicles offered a dome light as their only convenience item. Today panel trucks make unusual, but enjoyable, collector's vehicles.

feature that was now becoming outdated. In the heavy-duty models, where the D-series cab and high crowned fenders carried over, K-line styling features blended well and helped give these trucks a power image.

On the inside, the K-series cab represented nothing more than pure functionality, as if to say, "I'm here to work, not play." Take a look inside one of these trucks sometime and you'll see what I mean. The doors use steel for the liners around the door handles and window cranks, eliminating fiberboard or upholstered paneling that can soil or wear. The seat covering is durable grained Naugahyde, colored green regardless of body color. The only other interior covering is a fiberboard roof liner—also green. On K-line trucks, the dash instruments are placed in a rectangular display with gauges showing fuel level, generator output, water temperature, and oil pressure arranged around a rectangular-shaped speedometer. Knobs for headlights, choke, and other functions line the bottom of the dash's center section in groups of two on either side of center-positioned ignition switch. On the top of the dash a crank for opening the swing-out windshield sits just below the windshield divider bar. Another functional item, the dispatch box (called a glove box on a car) fits into the dash on the passenger side. A rubber mat covers the floor.

To put a K-line International truck cab's kindergarten-basic in perspective, it helps to

The most obvious differences between the K- and KB-series models are the "wings" on the sides of the grille, a wrap-around chrome piece on the front of the hood, and a hood ornament. Chrome lettering indicating the truck's model designation was also added just below the International nameplate on each side of the hood. A deluxe trim package could now be ordered as an option. Mechanical specifications were the same as for the K series.

remember that in the 1940s a light-duty truck wasn't anybody's idea of a commuting vehicle. On the farm, a pickup truck might be a family's only transportation, so Mom, Pop, and the kids would probably ride together in the truck to go shopping on Saturday and to church on Sunday. If the dog wanted to hop in for a ride too, nobody would get upset. Nor would anybody fuss much when sister Susie dropped her ice cream cone on the seat cushion; the durable Naugahyde could easily be wiped clean. With comfort ranking relatively low on a buyer's list of priorities, trucks were picked for the marks they scored on reliability and service.

Although light-duty K-series models look freshly restyled (let's remember that K-6 and larger trucks carried over the cab and fenders from the D line), the pickup box is only superficially different from that used on the D series. One of the easily noticeable changes, K-line pickups had a tube-type tailgate hinge, whereas the D- and earlier C-series pickup tailgates had strap hinges. On 113-inch short wheelbase K-1 pickups the box length measured 6 1/2 feet, while the 125-inch wheelbase K-1 and K-2 models had a 7 1/2-foot box. On 130-inch extended wheelbase K-3 pickups, an 8 1/2-foot box was used. In all cases, the pickup boxes shared a common width of 48 1/2 inches with 17-inch-high sideboards.

On some early post-war production K-series pickups, the box differs noticeably from normal IH production. These trucks were factory-equipped with a heavier duty aftermarket "Knox" box which is easily identified by its somewhat higher and thicker sides, checker-plate floor, and "Knox" stamped into the tailgate. (Some "Knox" boxes have a smooth tailgate.) The side panels on the "Knox" box also differ from IH production in that they lack the stiffening ribs found on factory box side panels. The "Knox" box was a carry-over item from wartime inventory (IH had contracted with Knox, a Knoxville, Tennessee, supplier, for boxes to install on a limited number of light-duty trucks that were built during the war). At war's end, the remaining boxes were placed on early production trucks. In wheat-belt states, buyers who got trucks with the Knox box valued its grain-tight tailgate.

Like pickups, panel trucks came in all three light-duty models: K-1, K-2, and K-3. This fully enclosed truck used welded steel construction with plywood flooring. The short 113-inch wheelbase version (offered only in the K-1 and K-2 load range) had a 7-foot-long cargo area. Panels built on the 125-inch wheelbase could carry items 8 feet in length, while the 130-inch wheelbase panels could accommodate cargo 9 feet in length. Since panel trucks typically served as delivery vehicles, they came standard-equipped with a single, adjustable bus-type seat for the driver. Buyers could add a second seat at extra cost. These no-frills vehicles offered a dome light as their only convenience feature. Other standard equipment items included a rearview mirror, electric windshield wiper on the driver's side only, stone guards on the rear fenders, tool box, and spare wheel. Also at extra cost, buyers could add a passenger side windshield wiper, rear bumper, tire for the spare wheel, and a chrome-plated windshield frame.

Along with several other manufacturers, International built a variant of the panel truck, called the canopy express, as a special purpose delivery and vending vehicle, used largely by fruit and vegetable peddlers. On the canopy express, the sides of the cargo area are open, allowing the peddler to display his areas. These openings could be covered by waterproof curtains attached by snaps to the flareboards and tailgate—thus protecting the vendor's wares from not just weather but also pilferage. Optionally, wire-mesh screens could be installed over open sides and rear, giving more security to the vendor's inventory and

adapting the truck for other uses, such as picking up stray animals. Because of the openings to the cargo area, the driver's compartment is fully enclosed, affording protection from the weather. Since this truck saw use mainly on produce farms, folding bench seats could be installed in the cargo area for transporting field workers. In the K series, canopy express models were offered in all light-duty series on the same chassis lengths as panel trucks. This model, which was not a big seller when new, is extremely rare today.

As in the D series, the wooden-bodied station wagon is the most attractive of all light-duty International K-line models. Two versions continued to be available, a seven-passenger model built on the 113-inch wheelbase and offered only in the K-1 range and a eleven-passenger wagon built on the 130-inch wheelbase and offered in the K-3 range. Both featured removable rear seats, a fold-down tailgate, a single door on the left side of the body for the driver and two doors on the right for passengers. The woody bodies were ruggedly built of quality hardwood, but even so, any woody wagon found "in the rough" today would most likely need extensive wood replacement, a job that requires a cabinet-maker's skills.

Stake/platform trucks were offered in all three light-duty models, but only on the longer wheelbases. The platform body had a welded-steel frame structure with an oak floor. K-1 and K-2 versions using the 125-inch wheelbase had a load length of 7-feet. The 130-inch wheelbase K-3 offered an 8-foot-long platform. It was common for these platform bodies to be fitted with removable stake racks, and International dealers could install a hinged end gate at extra cost.

Specification sheets show few differences between the K-1 and K-2 models. Variations in load rating were accomplished mainly by beefing up suspension components. The K-3, however, was an all-round beefier truck having a heavier frame, larger brakes, and a full-floating rear end that supported the axles on two roller bearings, as opposed to the single roller bearing on the K-1 and K-2 rear axles.

With the new Indianapolis engine plant now on a production footing, International could equip all its light-truck models with its own engines, which were, of course, the familiar L-head six whose design had been purchased from Willys. For the K series, International called this engine the Green Diamond and, indeed, a stamping of the company's Triple diamond logo, with the words Green Diamond in the center, appears on the left side of K-series engine blocks. Because economy was still a concern, this Green Diamond engine was available in two sizes: the standard 214 with a compression ratio of 6.3:1, and a maximum brake horsepower rating of 82.9 at 3,400 rpm, and a downsized 175-cubic inch economy version having a slightly higher 6.7:1 compression ratio, and a maximum brake horsepower rating of 64 at 3,300 rpm. Both engines used a single-barrel downdraft-type carburetor from Zenith, Carter, or Holley, with an oil-bath air cleaner as standard equipment.

All light-duty K-series trucks used the same transmission, an IHC-manufactured three-speed. On the prewar Ks, operators used a floor lever to shift gears, while 1946 and later production used a more convenient column shift. The floor-shift, four-speed "crash box" transmission from the medium-duty K-4 line could be optioned on all light Ks at an extra cost of $17.50. Veteran truckers remember this type of transmission without a great deal of fondness as a "double clutcher" because its straight-cut gears required depressing the clutch and revving the engine to synchronize engine rpm and speed at the rear wheels in order to avoid grinding the gears.

Driveline elements for light-duty K models consisted of the following in nearly any combination.

Standard	Optional
GRD 214 engine	GRD 175 economy engine
4.18 rear end	3.72 or 5.11 rear end gearing
3-speed HDS transmission	4-speed H-41 transmission

On the K-1 and K-2, 6.00x16 tires were standard, with oversize tires up to 7.50x16 available at extra cost. Other extra-cost equipment included a rear bumper, bumper guards, radio and radio antenna, cigar lighter, spotlight, fog lights, external sun shade, dual inside sun visors, clock, dual wipers, electric windshield wiper motor, heater/defroster, dual tail lights, turn signals, headlight beam indicator, chrome windshield frame, and chrome wheel-trim rings.

One of the less common, but highly useful, accessories was a NO ROL device that enabled the operator to hold a stopped truck with the clutch. After stopping the truck with the brake and depressing the clutch to shift into a lower gear, the NO ROL locks up the brakes allowing the operator to take his foot off the brake pedal to work the accelerator for starting the truck moving again. Without the NO ROL accessory, the driver has to do some fast footwork between the brake and accelerator, especially when starting out on a hill.

International provided its K-series trucks in six standard colors: red, dark green, black, gray, maroon, and blue. Chassis components, the frame, running boards, drivetrain, windshield frame, wheels, and engine accessories were painted black. As would be expected, the Green Diamond engine was painted green.

Shortly after the United States entered World War II in December 1941, production of cars and trucks for civilian use came to a halt. At Springfield and Fort Wayne, International built military trucks while the Indianapolis engine plant turned out engines for generators, armored vehicles, and assault craft, as well as trucks. In its other manufacturing facilities, IH built shells, bomb cases, and crawler tractors. Since International had little experience with all-wheel drive, its first military trucks were 4x2s and 6x4s. Before long, however, an all-wheel-drive system was designed and IHC built thousands more trucks in 4x4 and 6x6 configurations.

For the Navy, International built two light-duty military models, the M-1-4 1/2-ton and the M-2-4 1-ton. The M-1-4 used the K-1's 113-inch wheelbase and 214-cubic inch Green Diamond engine, with some being fitted with the larger 233-ci Green Diamond engine from the medium-duty line. This truck had 4x4 drive and rode on 9.00 x 16 tires. Both cargo and ambulance versions were built. The M-2-4 used the K-2's 125-inch wheelbase and the 233 Green Diamond engine. This model was also a 4x4 and was fitted with cargo bodies. International's military trucks served in all theaters of the war, from North Africa to Europe and from the Middle East to the Pacific. For its part in the war effort, International built 120,000 military trucks, including 13,000 M-14 and M-17 half-tracks.

To meet an increasingly critical truck shortage on the home front, in 1943, the War Production Board gave International permission to build a relatively small number (limited to 10% of the total output) of trucks for civilian use. With only a trickle of new trucks to sell, IHC dealerships survived by providing repair services. Most dealerships operated on a skeleton staff, most able-bodied men having been drafted or volunteered for the armed services.

Building trucks for war use taught IH many technical lessons and when civilian production resumed after the defeat of Germany and Japan in 1945, this knowledge was incorporated as

On some early post-war production K-series pickups, the box differs noticeably from normal IH production. These trucks were factory- equipped with a heavier duty aftermarket "Knox" box, which is easily identified by its somewhat higher and thicker sides and "Knox" stamped into the tailgate.

improvements into the company's heavy-duty trucks. Light trucks, however, remained essentially unchanged, except for the previously noted switch to column shift for the standard-equipment three-speed transmission.

In January 1947, International introduced its very modestly updated KB models. According to the ads that introduced the new models, the KB exhibited 95 features and improvements over the K series. This seems an exaggerated claim and if 95 changes did indeed occur, most are too minute for the average observer to notice. The most obvious differences between the K- and KB-series trucks are the "wings" on the sides of the grille, a wrap-around chrome piece on the front of the hood, and a hood ornament. Chrome lettering indicating the truck's model designation was also added just below the International nameplate on each side of the hood. A deluxe trim package could now be ordered as an option. Mechanical specifications were the same as for the K series, except for the discontinuation of the economy 175-cubic inch engine The economy engine had never been a big seller and with the pent-up demand for new trucks, International no longer needed to offer an engine that offered marginal performance just to shave a few pennies off fuel costs.

Throughout the 1940s, IHC placed fourth in light-truck sales behind Chevrolet, Ford, and Dodge, in that order. In 1941, International built its 1,000,000th truck. War production added another 122,000 and by 1947, International's total truck output reached 1 1/2 million. This rate of growth would not hold, however, and it would be 1956 before International's total truck production topped two million. In part, International's sales slip resulted from the increasingly keen competition, led by Chevrolet's all-new "Advance Design" trucks in 1947, Ford's "Bonus Built" truck line, introduced in 1948, Dodge's "Pilot House Cab" truck line that appeared the same year, and Studebaker's modern styled and well engineered R series of 1949. As these rapid-fire developments were occurring, International held on to a well-engineered but increasingly dated-looking truck line that had first appeared in 1940.

chapter seven

1950-1952 L SERIES:
Trucks with
"The Roomiest Cab on the Road"

"New from bumper to taillight." That's how International's ads heralded the company's L-line trucks when they were introduced to the public in October 1949. While automotive advertising has been known for overstatement, in this case the claim was valid. Not only had the styling been brought up to date, but the engines, chassis, suspension, and even the brakes had been redesigned. The L line represented such a sweeping change that on the light-duty trucks, about the only parts carried over from the preceding KB models were the hub caps on the 1/2 tons, plus one of the three-speed transmissions.

In total, the L line consisted of 66 models in load ranges from 1/2 ton to six-wheelers with GVW ratings of 20 tons. Where most truck makers offered three light-duty models, International now offered nine. This expanded lineup allowed customers to purchase a truck exactly tailored to their needs. In the light-duty range, International fielded three 1/2-ton models: the L110 with a GVW of 4,200 pounds, the L111 with a 4,500-pound GVW, and the L112 with a 4,800-pound GVW rating; three 3/4-ton models: the L-120 with a 5,200-pound GVW, the L-121 rated at 5,700 pounds GVW, and the L-122 carrying a 6,200-pound GVW; plus three "tonner" trucks: the L-130 with a GVW of 6,800 pounds, the L-131, rated at 7,400 pounds GVW, and the L-132 having an 8,000-pound GVW. Chrome numbers on

> The L-line cab's one-piece curved windshield represented an International first. In 1950 when these trucks were introduced, only a few luxury class cars offered a curved, one-piece windshield, and no other trucks.

the side of the cowl below the International nameplate tell the truck's model designation.

The ads also claimed the new L-series trucks to have "The roomiest cab on the road." With an inside width of 58 1/4 inches an L-series cab could still be a tight fit for three large men, but two men, or a man, woman, and child could sit side-by-side quite comfortably. Not only was the seat wider, but the roomier cab also allowed for 4 inches of travel in seat adjustment. The track on which the seat mounted canted up at an angle toward the front so that as the seat moved forward it also elevated the seating position. Conversely, moving the seat back lowered the seating position. Thus, in adjusting the seat the driver wasn't just gaining or decreasing leg room. He was also adjusting the seating position in relation to his body height. In all previous International trucks the seat had been nonadjustable, so the new design made a big improvement in driver comfort.

The L-line cab gave attention to driver and passenger comfort by providing vent windows that could be opened to deflect fresh air onto the truck's occupants. A second fresh-air source, from a ventilator scoop on the cowl, could be opened to cool the cab floor. For cold weather operation, two heaters were now available, a new fresh-air type that ducted outside air across the heater core, and the older recirculating type that heated air already inside the truck.

International's designers did a masterful job in preserving a clear styling link between the K and L-series trucks. While the wide front fenders, broad "mustache" grille and flat hood give the L series a more modern lower look, the sculpted lines that ran along the sides of the hood on the K and KB models can also be found on the L series.

Besides roominess and comfort, the new cab greatly increased glass area for improved visibility and safety. The cab's one-piece curved windshield represented an International first. In 1950, only a few luxury-class cars offered a curved, one-piece windshield, and no other trucks. The two-piece rear window provided substantially better visibility than the small rear glass of the K series and the rear window's center post is not as much of an obstacle to rear-ward vision as it might seem since truckers customarily view the world behind them through their side-view mirrors. Larger windows in the doors also contributed to the cab's improved visibility.

In spite of these advances, the inside of an International truck cab was still quite Spartan. Fiberboard panels now covered the access openings to the window mechanism in the doors, but arm rests were omitted unless the buyer selected them at extra cost. Buyers also paid extra for a dome light, passenger-side sun visor, cigar lighter, electric windshield wipers (vacuum wipers were standard), a lock for the glove compartment, foam-rubber seat padding, and side-view mirrors. For operators who wanted entertainment, an AM radio could be optioned.

The instrument panel followed the cab's curved windshield contour. Instruments now sat in circular housing beside an identically housed speedometer. A push button on the dash replaced the floor-mounted, kick-type starter switch of

earlier International trucks, while chrome knobs, located toward the center of the dash, worked the lights, choke, heater, and other controls. A chromed ash tray occupied the dash's center location, above the optionally installed radio. When the buyer specified a three-speed transmission, the shift lever mounted on the steering column. Four-speed transmissions used a floor shift.

The L line's complete external redesign brought several changes that have been highly appreciated by these trucks' owners. Perhaps the most notable is the dual hinge/latch hood. Through a cleverly designed latching mechanism that could also act as a hinge, International's engineers made it possible to open the truck's hood from either side, or if both sets of hinges were unlatched, to lift the hood entirely off the truck. The ability to open the hood from either side, or remove it entirely, made the truck's engine and related equipment fully accessible, whether to routine maintenance and service or major repair and overhaul.

Probably the single most telltale feature identifying a 1950s International as an L model is the grille, which consists of a series of short vertical grille openings over two long horizontal bars. At extra cost the horizontal bars could be chromed; however, these bars were painted body color as standard equipment. To many, the vertical openings, which are shorter toward the headlights, resemble a brush mustache. It's a design no other manufacturer ever chose to imitate.

Another distinguishing feature, the bumpers on L-line trucks are channel style (as opposed to the spring-steel bumpers on KB and earlier International light trucks). Although International supplied painted bumpers as standard equipment, chrome-plated front and rear bumpers were available at extra cost. Early L models had concealed door hinges, but in 1951 externally visible hinges were used and these detracted slightly from the otherwise smooth cab lines. The protruding hinge offered an ideal mounting location of the side-view mirror, which on 1950 models attached to the cowl just below the windshield pillar. Since external changes were virtually nonexistent for the L line, the visible door hinges and hinge-mounted side mirror a1952 L-model truck from a 1950.

As mentioned earlier, significant mechanical changes also occurred with the L series. Perhaps the most significant mechanical change came in the form of a new Silver Diamond six-cylinder engine with overhead valves. So different was the new engine that only ignition parts interchange with the former Green Diamond engine that traced its ancestry to Willys. The Silver Diamond boosted displacement to 220 ci, (compared to 214 for the Green Diamond) and upped the horsepower to 100 (compared to the former 82). The Silver Diamond block had an extremely rugged lower casting that extended below the center line of the crankshaft. Ford adopted a similar design for its overhead valve six and V-8 engines in the mid-fifties and used the terms "I" and "Y" block to describe the deep castings. These terms are sometimes also used to describe International's overhead-valve six and later V-8 engines of the same era. Due to the high torque curve at low speeds, an L pickup with the Silver Diamond overhead-valve engine can be idled down to 10 miles per hour in high gear and accelerated without bucking.

International's engineers made numerous changes to improve the riding qualities of their light trucks. Attaching the rear-spring mounts on the outside of the frame rails rather than to the bottom of the frame provided for longer spring travel, and increasing the distance between the springs also helped reduce lean on turns. In the front, the shackles were now placed at the rear of the springs to reduce road shock. The use of rubber for spring and shackle bushings helped reduce vibration and eliminated the need to lubricate the spring mounts. Consequently, grease fittings were omitted in these locations. Slightly longer springs were installed front and rear for greater springing action and in early 1950 the number of spring leafs was reduced from nine to seven as another step toward a smoother ride. With the L series, International switched to new style double-action shock absorbers because of the improvement these tube type (also called airplane type) shocks made in vehicle stability and riding qualities.

Chassis changes weren't limited to suspension improvements. The distance between the frame rails was also altered to meet the SAE-standardized 34-inch frame channel width that allowed easy mounting of after-market utility and wrecker bodies, and enabled buyers to use a stake rack, or other specialty body from another truck on his new International. Other light-truck manufacturers had adopted the SAE frame standards on their redesigned postwar models. International had lagged in adopting the standardized frame width, because the KB frame carried over from the K models.

Other underbody changes included moving the gas tank to an outboard location on the left side of the frame and placing the steering box ahead of the front axle. The more forward location of the steering box put the steering wheel at a more comfortable angle for the driver while increasing the steering mechanism's leverage for easier steering and improved handling. Brakes were now self-energizing, meaning that frequent adjustments were no longer needed to maintain a firm-feeling brake pedal. Improvements in the form of rear fender braces and different radiator supports, to name but two examples, continued throughout the L series.

L-series pickup boxes are wider and deeper boxes than those on previous models. Width between the sidewalls now measured 54 1/2 inches, so the wheelwells protruded slightly into the box. However, a 48 1/2-inch width of flat floor between the wheelwells still made it possible to stack 4-by-8-foot sheets of building materials on the box floor. The side boards measured 19 inches to the top of the horizontal flare boards. To make L-series pickups easily identifiable from the rear, the tailgate now displayed the International name in raised block letters.

Short (115-inch) wheelbase pickups in the 1/2-ton L110 and 3/4-ton L122 models carried a 6 1/2-foot box, while long (127-inch) wheelbase trucks were fitted with the 8-foot box. In keeping with its greater load capacity, the 134-inch wheelbase L-130 model had a 9-foot box; this model could be equipped with dual-rear wheels which required extra-wide rear fenders. Short wheelbase pickups mounted the spare tire on the left side of the box, with a portion of the tire fitting into a recess in the rear fender. Longer wheelbase pickups carried the spare tire on the right side of the box. Since the longer wheelbase allows space for the tire to fit between the cab and rear fender, on those trucks the rear fender is not recessed for the tire. On both short and long wheelbase models, the running boards were now extended all the way to the rear fenders.

L-series panel trucks were built on the 115-inch wheelbase and offered as L110 and L120 models. Taking a cue from Chevrolet, which built a passenger van called the Carryall Suburban based on its panel-truck body, International began development of an all-metal passenger van, called the Travelall, based on the panel-body shell. Officially, Travelalls did not enter production until 1953 with the R series. International truck researcher and historian Robert Chaney maintains, however, that Travelalls were built in the L series, but their sale and distribution limited to fleet purchases by the U.S. military, specifically the Air Force. Chaney reports obtaining parts from Travelalls having L-series styling features, all of which, he notes, were originally painted bright yellow and

"Roomiest cab on the road." That's how International's ad writers described the completely redesigned L-line pickup cab. Note that the curved dash follows the windshield contour. All instruments are grouped into two gauges and controls are placed within easy reach of the driver. *Courtesy of* This Old Truck *magazine*

had U.S. Air Force markings. Further, these L-series Travelalls differed from later R- and S-series trucks in that they had panel-board door-insert panels and full instrumentation, features lacking on R- and S-series Travelalls, which shared the L-line body shell.

Chaney's conclusion is that the Travelall was initially sold as a military vehicle and became available to civilians only after the end of the Korean Conflict in 1953, by which time International had launched its R series.

Although International continued to offer a light-duty cowl and chassis on which woody station wagons could be mounted through the L and into the R series, very few International trucks of this body style were sold. By 1950 wooden-bodied station wagons had nearly become obsolete, replaced by the increasingly popular Travelall-type all-metal passenger vans, but obsoleted also by the woody body's requirement of frequent care and maintenance. Besides utility, the woody station wagon's attraction had been its appearance. It had been a great image vehicle for resort hotels who would run these picturesque transports to train depots to pick up and deliver guests. With the decline in train travel, resort hotels found their guests delivering themselves to the hotel door and what had been a small, but steady market for woody station wagons disappeared. Other buyers, such as schools and construction companies were as well served by the new all-metal passenger vans and busses.

For schools needing a transport vehicle smaller than a standard-sized, truck-based school bus, International offered a bus body on the light-duty chassis. In the days of decentralized schools, these small busses were an efficient way to transport children to the one- or two-room schools in their districts.

Besides the pickup, panel, fleet-production Travelalls, woody station wagon, and small school bus, International continued to make its light-duty trucks available in cab-chassis configurations on which a variety of specialty bodies, as well as familiar and functional platform/stake bodies, were mounted.

Due to the L line's thoughtful development, International had been able to enter the 1950s—a fiercely competitive decade—with a strong product. The L line's styling proved sufficiently advanced for the basic sheet metal to be used through the middle of the decade on the R and S models, while the overhead valve Silver Diamond engine served through the end of International's light-duty truck line in 1975. Furthermore, the changes that had been made to suspension and chassis design strengthened International's already strong reputation for reliability and ruggedness. Simply put, the L-series trucks were strong, well styled for the era, and a suitable platform for future development.

The wider lines of the L-series styling added more interior space to the panel body, which became the shell from which the Travelall was created.

chapter eight

R AND S SERIES:
"Built As Only IH Can Build 'Em!"

Because appearance changes were minimal, the 1953–1955 R line is best remembered as a transition series that introduced the Travelall and Metroette, as well as numerous mechanical advances. Basically, the Travelall was a passenger van created by adding windows, seats and additional side doors to a panel truck. It was a vehicle of great practicality and became popular not only with farm families already loyal to International trucks and agricultural equipment, but also with mining companies, airports, the park service, and a wide variety of businesses that needed a rugged transport that could carry a gang of people.

In the Metroette, International offered a delivery van built on a standard light truck chassis. This new delivery model was not intended as a replacement for the Metro delivery van which it had introduced in 1939 and would remain in production through 1964. Rather, as the name suggests, International slotted the Metroette for businesses needing a delivery van with smaller capacity than the Metro. Also, because the Metroette had a relatively high-volume production chassis as its base, it was less expensive than the Metro. International offered the Metroette only in the R-120 series as the RA-120 model.

The easiest way to recognize an L-series truck is by the grille, which consisted of an oval opening crossed by a single bar carrying a modernized IH emblem in its center, and an air intake at the front of the hood. Cab dimensions and styling stayed the same and pickup trucks continued the novel two-piece rear window.

> Most International truck fanciers also prefer red (IH) tractors.

In 1954 International added two more light-duty pickup models, the R-100 and R-102. Both used the short 115-inch wheelbase and were fitted with the 6 1/2-foot box. The R-100 and the slightly heavier duty R-102 supplemented, rather than replaced, the R-110 model. In fact, the specifications show very few differences between the R-100 and R-110 1/2-ton pickups. Both carried a GVW rating of 4,200 pounds and used the same 220-ci Silver Diamond engine. As a lighter-duty truck, the R-100 rode on 6.70x15 four-ply tires, while the R-110 continued to use 6.00x16 six-ply rubber. As noted, the R-100 and R-102 were available only on the short wheelbase, while the R-110, R-111, and R-112 1/2-ton models were built on both 115- and 127-inch wheelbases.

With five different models in the 1/2-ton class alone, International was essentially building trucks on a custom basis to meet the needs of the individual customer. It was a great concept, and one that no doubt some, if not all, truck builders will soon revisit. However, such a proliferation of models created difficulties in service, particularly when replacement parts were needed. The model number alone didn't tell, for certain, which transmission, rear axle, propeller shaft, or other mechanical components had been used in configuring a given truck. Moving up the light-duty range, this same proliferation of models also existed in the 3/4 and 1-ton classes. In the R-120 (3/4-ton) class buyers could choose between the R-120, R-121, and R-122 models. While all three trucks used the

Apart from minor styling changes, most notably to the grille and hood, the R-series models are a continuation of the L line, even including the split window at the rear of the cab. R-110 models, like this one owned by George Mitchell, carried the same 1/2-ton rating as the R-100, but as a lighter-duty truck, the R-100 rode on 6.70x15 four-ply tires. The R-110 continued to use 6.00x16 six-plies.

The block letter International emblem continues from the D series. Note the separate emblem showing the model designation.

same 220-ci Silver Diamond engine and 6.50x16 six-ply tires, differences appeared in load rating (the R-120 carried a GVW rating of 5,400 pounds, while the R-121 had a 5,900-pound GVW rating and the R-122 a 6,500-pound rating), wheelbase lengths (115 and 127 inches), and rear axle ratios (4.1 and 4.777), among others. Available body types in the R-120 class included the pickup, panel, stake, cab/chassis, school bus, and Metroette.

The 1-ton R-130 continued this model proliferation models with the R-130 (6,800-pound GVW), the R-131 (7,700-pound GVW), and the R-132 (8,600-pound GVW) offered on two wheelbases, 115 and 134 inches. Body types in the R-130 class were limited to the pickup and stake/platform, plus a cab/chassis on which a variety of special bodies could be mounted. Rear axle ratios at this upper end of the light-duty scale ranged from 4.3 to 1 to a stump pulling 6.166 to 1.

Besides two new models, the Travelall and Metroette, and expansion of light-duty models to nearly a build-to-suit range of options, R line also brought numerous mechanical upgrades and developments, including four-wheel drive and an automatic transmission. As would be expected

International's light-duty R-series trucks were available with platform-stake bodies, which gave added space for bulky items like apple boxes or hay bales.

from International, its four-wheel-drive system was an integrated design and not an add-on. Unlike Ford and Chevrolet four-wheel drive of the mid-1950s, both of which were add-on systems that required noticeable chassis elevation, International retained nearly the standard two-wheel drive truck's load height. International also built its four-wheel drive with power-takeoff, a very useful function to farmers, utility companies, and many others whose vehicle specifications called for off-road capability.

In late 1954 when International offered an automatic transmission for its light-duty trucks, the choice was a GM-built Hydra-Matic. First made available in GMC trucks in 1953, the truck Hydra-Matic had already proven itself capable of rough use. In addition to being

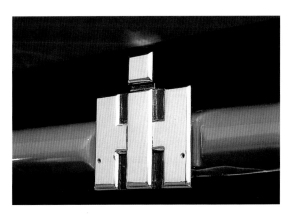

International would use the block letter IH emblem that debuted with the R series until the sale of its agricultural equipment line to Case and selection of Navistar as the new corporate name in the mid-1980s.

Instrumentation on R-series trucks is complete and easily readable.

The dash places all controls within easy reach of the driver. Note the two-tone color scheme.

reliable, the dual-range Hydra-Matic is a fairly efficient transmission, at least by the standards of early automatics. To help compensate for the power loss inherent in any automatic, the Silver Diamond also received a slight power boost (to 108 horsepower) due to a slightly higher 7:1 compression ratio resulting from the use of domed pistons.

The R series continued the hood latch arrangement whereby the hood could be opened from either side and removed from the truck by releasing the latches on both sides. To point out one small difference, on R trucks the hood latches were painted (the latches had been chrome

plated on L-line trucks), with chromed latches now an extra-cost item. Instruments on R-line trucks placed the IH insignia in the center of the gauge. The ignition key now engaged the starter instead of the push button used with the L line. In late 1954, tubeless tires became standard equipment. The entire automotive and light truck industry made this switch from tube-type to tubeless tires to speed up the tire-mounting process on the assembly line.

With the exception of the hood handles, the standard and optional equipment lists carried over from the L series essentially unchanged. Included in the vehicle base price were an ash tray, right-side door lock, rubber floor mat, left-hand side-view mirror, sun visor on the driver's side, dual vacuum windshield wipers, spare tire, and a jack and handle. Optional extra-cost equipment included a dome light, right and left side arm rests, rearview mirror, passenger side sun visor, foam-padded seat, chrome-plated front or rear bumper, the chromed hood handles, green-tinted windshield, fresh air or recirculating type heater and defroster, dual electric windshield wipers, an AM radio, clock, cigar lighter, lockable glove compartment, turn signals, power steering, an engine governor, oil filter, heavy-duty clutch, and overload springs.

In 1955, the R series' final year, several design changes occurred to truck cabs that may go overlooked unless you should happen to see an early and late R-series truck parked side by side. The most noticeable of these changes and the easiest way to spot a 1955 R truck is the larger one-piece rear window. Less noticeable are the deeper side windows in the doors and push-button type outside door handles. Changes on the inside of the cab included metal inner door panels replacing the former cardboard panels and a redesigned steering column that enclosed the shifting linkage for the three-speed transmission. The extra-cost equipment list for light-duty trucks now showed the Black Diamond 240-ci engine.

Also in 1955, International followed the rest of the industry in offering two-tone paint schemes on its light duty trucks. The most common combination used Magnolia Ivory with a solid color such as Red, Blue, Yellow, Tan, but two-toning could also be done with light and dark shades of the same color such as Cascade Green and Adirondack Green or Yuma Cream and Adobe Tan. On trucks with two-toning, the lighter color was applied to the upper portion of the vehicle. The dividing line between the colors followed from the edges of the front fenders (the

The bumper guards and chrome bumper shown on this truck were an accessory. A plain painted bumper was standard.

R-series trucks are recognized by the grille, which consisted or an oval opening crossed by a single bar carrying the modernized IH emblem in the center. Trucks in this series continued the hood latch arrangement whereby the hood could be opened from either side or removed from the truck by releasing the latches on both sides.

Although S-series trucks carried over the R line's sheet metal nearly intact, there are differences, most noticeably in the grille, front fenders, and hood. The quickest recognition test is the location of the headlights, which on the S series sit in the front fender crowns.

hood received the lighter color) to the belt line above the door handles on the sides of the cab. On Travelalls, the color line followed the belt line all the way around the vehicle.

International advertised its R series as the ". . . most complete truck line, built as only IH can build 'em." Counting all models, light and heavy-duty, a total of 168 different trucks were offered. The R line also upheld International's tradition for ruggedness and dependability. In 1955, a record-setting sales year for the entire industry, International's truck sales rose by a whopping 37 percent, positioning the company solidly in the No. 3 position among U.S. truck builders.

Another S Series

It's unlikely that many buyers of the S-series trucks International built between late 1955 and early spring 1957 remembered the earlier S line of 1921–1929 that had been such a sales success that it had made International a major manufacturer of light-duty trucks. The second S series didn't make any strong statements, either in styling or in new models. Basically, International used the S series to keep the basic L and R design in production one

International chose the R line to enter the light-duty four-wheel-drive market. Because four-wheel drive is generally associated with hard use, this maximum traction option was fitted to the heavier duty R-120, as well as the larger R-140 and R-160 models.

Although the taller 9.00x16 eight-ply tires gave a slightly higher stance, International boasted that the loading height on its 4x4 pickups was only three inches higher than the 2x4 models. An S-series 4x4 pickup is shown here.

more year in anticipation of the sweepingly reworked A-line trucks that would celebrate International's Golden Anniversary of truck building.

Although the S-series trucks carried over the R line's sheet metal nearly intact, there are differences: most noticeably in the grille, front fenders, and hood. The quickest recognition test is the location of the headlights, which on the S series sit in the front fender crowns instead of beside the grille where they had been on the L and R lines. The shape of the grille is also different, the grille opening now having a trapezoid-shape. The parking lights, which in the S series are round, sit inside the grille enclosure. The air scoop in the front of the hood has a lower profile and extends nearly across the front of the hood. The hood also has a flatter profile and flares out to meet the front fenders.

Other changes are less noticeable. The lightest duty S-100 and S-102 models used an economy version of the Silver Diamond engine, now detuned to 100 horsepower, while the S-110 to S-130 trucks had the 240-ci Black Diamond engine from the medium-duty range. The S-100 was available only with the short 115-inch wheelbase and the Travelall was now offered in

both the S-100 and S-120 lines. In the R series the Travelall had been offered only as a 110 model. The Travelall received the same styling updates as pickups, namely new front fenders, grille, and hood, as well as the taller windshield and deeper door windows that had appeared toward the end of the R run. The rear portion of the Travelall body retained the shallower windows of the early R and L series, so the overall look is not exactly integrated.

Standard equipment items on S-series trucks were little changed from the R series, except that a fresh-air heater, dome light, and oil filter were now installed at no extra cost. On the option side, the four-speed was now all synchromesh and buyers could select a 12-volt, negative-ground electrical system. (The standard electrical system was 6-volt, positive ground.)

The S series lasted only a little over a year and succeeded in its primary function of keeping International in third place on the sales charts. But to remain competitive, major changes were needed, and what better time to introduce those changes than on the celebration of 50 years as a truck builder.

The four-wheel-drive option was especially popular with farmers, who were already among the more loyal buyers of International trucks. This ad features International's 1959 truck models.

So well executed was the original design that with few and relatively minor changes, the Metro moved from the D to the K and KB series and on to the L, R, and S lines. The 1953 RM 150 Metro shown here is owned by George Mitchell.

International Harvester Adds 4wd to Its Light-Duty Truck Line

From the 1920s to the 1950s, International Harvester (usually abbreviated IH) ranked among the leaders in light-truck sales. Distinctive styling and a nearly legendary reputation for reliability fostered an owner loyalty that resulted in many truck operators never having owned another make besides International. Primarily large truck and farm equipment manufacturer, International Harvester built all its products for hard work—its pickups included. So it followed that when IH decided to enter the four-wheel-drive market with its new R-line models, introduced in 1953, it offered this maximum traction option its heavier-duty R-120 3/4-ton trucks, as well as the larger R-140 and R-160 1-ton models.

International's R-line trucks had a non-flamboyant, functional appearance that incorporated several useful features, including a hood that could be opened from either side, or removed entirely simply by releasing the latches on both sides of the hood, and key ignition as on today's

trucks, and were available with both automatic transmission and power steering. In addition to four wheelbase choices (115, 122, 127, or 134-inches), when a buyer specified a 4x4, he also gained two engine options. For the R line, the standard 220-ci Silver Diamond engine received a power increase from 100 to 108 horsepower. Also available with four-wheel drive was the 240-ci Black Diamond (really a medium-duty truck engine) rated at 131 horsepower. This optional engine could also be converted to run on LP gas.

Unlike Ford and Chevrolet 4wd conversions, which in the 1950s mounted the transfer case remote from the transmission, for its four-wheel-drive models, International attached the transfer case to the rear of the transmission, giving its 4x4 pickups a loading height only three inches higher than its 2x4 models. Another advantage, particularly for trucks used on farms, International's two-speed transfer case also made provision for a power take-off hookup that could operate a winch, hydraulic hoist, and various other pieces of equipment, including water pumps and agricultural

The driver's controls are simple and conveniently placed, as might be expected in a delivery vehicle. The original condition of Mitchell's Metro can be seen by the worn spot on the floor, where the truck's driver rested his left foot.

machinery. IH 4x4 pickups could be fitted with 6 1/2- foot, 8-foot, or 9-foot boxes, depending on wheelbase length, or stake or platform bodies could be installed. In anticipation of rugged use, IH equipped its 4x4 light-duty trucks with 9.00x16 eight-ply tires as standard equipment.

In 1957, with the introduction of its Golden Anniversary A line, International extended four-wheel drive to its Travelall, a truck-based people transporter similar to the Chevrolet Suburban. As would be expected, four-wheel-drive Travelalls were fitted with stiffer springs, resulting in a harsher ride than the two-wheel-drive models, and were intended for use in regions where roads were primitive or nonexistent. Another four-wheel-drive model, the Travelette crew cab pickup, combined the passenger hauling capacity of a Travelall with the cargo space of a pickup. Although crew cab pickups have since become quite popular, this model was an International first.

As American truck builders expanded, their range of light-duty 4wd offerings no one but farmers and other primarily off-road operators seemed to take notice. Some spark of interest appeared needed to ignite the public's awareness of the fun, as well as the traction and multi-purpose opportunities offered by four-wheel drive. That spark came in 1961 with International's introduction of its 4x4 utility vehicle, the Scout. Immediately Scout sales soared to records neither IH nor anyone else in the industry had anticipated. The Scout's success birthed a new class of vehicles whose popularity in the 1990s enabled trucks to overtake cars for America's best selling vehicles—something never remotely imagined in the early development of 4wd.

While light-duty Metro models used a column mounted gearshift, the heavier-duty trucks had a floor shift.

chapter nine

1957-1960 A AND B SERIES:
IH Marks 50 Years As a Truck Builder

One might ask why International followed the S series with the A series; why not a T series? The answer is simple: A stood for Anniversary.

When GM restyled its trucks in 1955, the new cab wore a styling feature that virtually overnight became *de rigueur* in the automotive industry. That styling feature was, as anyone who remembers the 1950s era will recognize, the wraparound windshield. The public had first seen wraparound windshields on Motorama dream cars, and now that same aircraft canopy styling feature had been made available on a truck. Further, the company's barrage of advertising as well as salesmen at the local Chevy and GM truck dealerships insisted that the wraparound windshield wasn't just a styling gimmick, but a safety feature that eliminated the blind spots in the forward field of view caused by the windshield pillars. Of course, most of the wraparound windshield's safety claims were advertising hype, because whatever visibility had been gained was lost in distortion caused by the tight curvature at the wraparound point in the glass. Within a few years, the windshield pillars returned more or less to their rearward sloping position. The reason for talking at some length about this 1950s styling feature is to explain how International's A series, and the lines that followed through 1968, came to be endowed with the most panoramic windshield in the industry. The thinking of International's

> Features of the B-Line trucks were quad headlights and a mesh grille. The most significant new feature was the availability of International's rugged V-8 engines in the light-duty truck line.

truck stylists most likely went like this: If we can't be first, we can at least be bold.

None of the styling trends of the 1950s was subtle. Paint schemes favored soft pastels and two-toning, chrome and bright metal gave a tinsel look not just to cars of the period, but also to heavily optioned trucks. With its light-duty A-line models, International played "me too" on these features. Joining traditional truck colors like "Cornbinder" red were feminine two-tones like pink and white. (One wonders how Joe Rancher explained his selection of a pink truck to the boys at the Roadside Cafe.) In glitter, too, what with optional bright-metal bumpers, grille, headlight bezels, windshield molding—and side trim spears on trucks with two-toning— International qualified for the most "with it" competition.

This isn't to suggest that all of International's styling changes could be counted as superficial. The new cabs had a lower ground height, so running boards could be eliminated, and were wider, now providing comfortable three-abreast seating for adults. The glass area of the door windows and rear window also increased giving near 360-degree visibility. The Travelall's sweeping expanse of side window glass made this model a virtual green house.

Despite the changes, International managed to preserve a clear styling link with its earlier R- and S-series trucks. As examples: the scoop at the front of the hood, now widened to extend the full

Pioneers of Progress in truck manufacturing in 1907, and producers of the world's most complete line today, the Motor Truck Division of International Harvester Company signalizes its golden anniversary and the start of its second half-century of quality leadership by presenting a new, dramatically Action-Styled, mechanically perfected line of light, medium and heavy-duty trucks.

The International A-line, replacing the favorably received S-line, includes a complete range of conventional, cab-forward, forward-control and four-wheel-drive models. Entirely new are six-wheelers and six-wheel-drive models of cab-forward design.

Light-Duty Conventional Models

Completely restyled, these are offered in four series that comprise eight models. The A-100 Series pickups and TRAVELALLS, designed to do double duty in family use, are exceptionally easy riding and easy to drive. The A-110 Series models are excellent all-purpose half-ton chassis available with a variety of bodies. Completing the full range of light-duty service are the progressively higher rated models in the A-120 and A-130 Series with maximum GVW up to 8,800 pounds for Model A-132.

Pickup Bodies. Available for all models is a standard 7-foot pickup body as pictured on the cover. A Custom 7-foot pickup, illustrated above, is offered in combination with the Custom cab. These have bonus-load-space maximum inside width of 54½ inches. There is also an 8½-foot bonus-load-space pickup.

2

To celebrate its 50th anniversary as a truck builder, International released a limited edition "Golden Anniversary Special." This fancy A-100 pickup, with its two-tone paint scheme, smooth-sided box, and extensive use of bright metal trim, is one of the rarest and most desirable of all International pickups.

width of the grille; the trapezoid shaped grille, which carried over from 1956; and the winged IH emblem, now perched boldly above the grille opening, all saying to buyers and bystanders alike that this was the new International.

Starring in the lineup of A-series pickups that appeared in early spring of 1957 was a slab-sided,

custom-trim pickup. Though manufacturers like Crosley had built pickups with cargo boxes that blended smoothly with the cab as early as the 1940s, it was General Motors that popularized the smooth-sided pickup box with its Motorama styled 1955 Chevrolet Cameo and GMC Suburban pickups. But despite their external appearance, the boxes on these trucks were not really wide-box designs; rather they were old-style narrow boxes covered with fiberglass fenders that gave the smooth-sided look. International followed the same approach with its slab-sided "Golden Anniversary Special." On the inside, the smooth-side pickup box has the same dimensions as the fendered style. The only difference is the absence of holes for the fender bolts in the side panels; the outer skins fasten to the box with screws! The tailgate is a stock narrow-box item, camouflaged on the outside with a sheet metal covering. The use of a latch instead of chains and hooks to lock the tailgate made it possible to open the tailgate with one hand—a real convenience feature. International marked its "Golden Anniversary Special" custom models with a sweeping side molding and two-tone paint schemes. The smooth sided "Custom" pickup bodies appeared only in the 1957–1958 A series and are extremely rare today.

For the A series, International lengthened its traditional full-fender style short pickup box from 6 1/2 to 7 feet; likewise, the 8-foot-long box was lengthened to 8 1/2 feet. The rear fenders on these boxes are marked by a crease above the wheel cutout and a more angular shape. The absence of running boards led International to place short steps between the cab and rear fender so that operators would have a place to stand when loading or removing items from the front of the box.

Travelalls were available in the A-100 (1/2-ton) and A-120 (3/4-ton) models with a four-wheel-drive version offered only in the A-120 series. Along with substantially larger windows for greatly improved side and rear, as well as forward visibility, the completely redesigned Travelall added the convenience of a third door, placed behind the front passenger door on the same side. With two-tone paint and chromed trim, the Travelall now looked more like an all-purpose station wagon than a people-hauling truck—which, of course, was exactly International's intention.

Whereas the Travelall had originally been created by cutting side windows into a panel truck, now the panel looked like a Travelall with blanked in windows (the stamping cut-outs could clearly be seen in the sides of the panel body). Completing the Travelall resemblance, panel trucks could be ordered with the second door on the passenger side and extra side windows. Unlike the Travelall, which had a rear tailgate/liftgate, the panel came standard equipped with swing-out rear doors.

New to the A series was a Travelette crew cab pickup that combined the Travelall's people carrying capability with the cargo hauling capacity of a pickup. Although crew cab pickups have come to be quite popular, this idea was an International first. To keep the Travelette's overall length within a maneuverable 210 inches, the shorter 7-foot Custom pickup box was used. With its 129-inch wheelbase, this six-man pickup looked rather ungainly, but in fact it had a shorter overall length than many 1957 cars. International offered the Travelette as both an A-110 and A-120 model. Four-wheel drive was available in the A-120 model and was a popular option for Travelettes purchased for field operation and construction use.

Besides styling changes and new models, the A series added engineering improvements including a negative ground 12-volt electrical system (which had been optional on the S series). The increased voltage made a remarkable improvement in starting, so much so that the Black Diamond 240 and 264 sixes are amazingly easy to start even in sub-zero temperatures. The second major improvement, which occurred through a redesign of the cylinder head, applied to all three sixes (the Silver Diamond 220 and Black Diamond 240 and 264) and resulted in better valve life and greater combustion efficiency.

In an attempt to improve riding qualities, International's engineers lengthened the front springs on A-series light-duty trucks. This change didn't entirely count as an improvement. The longer springs changed the location of the front axle and in so doing placed more of the weight of the engine and nose portion of the truck ahead of the axle's center line. As a result of this out-front weight, the steering felt heavier (the truck required more effort to turn) and handling (which was never a truck's high point) degenerated. When International introduced a V-8 in its 1959 B series, the shorter engine helped correct the weight balance problem, improving both steering and handling.

The use of two-color vinyl for the seat upholstery, door panels, and sun visors, as well as the use of a color accent on the dash panel, gave A-line interiors a richer look than International's previous truck series. To make the cab more comfortable in both cold and hot weather, vent ducts built into cab structure routed outside air either to a fresh air outlet on left side near the clutch pedal or to the new-design fresh-air heater located under the dash on the passenger side. These air vents had baffles to keep out moisture, plus a drain at each side that exits in front of the door. A

All-steel, heavily insulated, weather-tight A-110 and A-120 panel trucks have adopted the attractive TRAVELALL styling. Extra right side door and extra side windows are optional.

Dramatically restyled, the exclusive, low-cost International A-100 or A-110 TRAVELALL accommodates up to 8 comfortable passengers, doubles as half-ton load carrier, has varied uses anywhere.

The A-line's squared-off styling looked good on both the panel and Travelall. For ease of entry and exit for rear-seat passengers, the Travelall added a second door on the passenger side.

benefit to the center passenger, the cab floor on A-series light-duty trucks is nearly flat with only a low hump for the drivetrain tunnel. A seemingly minor, yet progressive detail, the clutch and brake pedals were now the overhead-suspended "swing" type that not only eliminated the drafty holes in the floor, but also moved the brake master cylinder to a more accessible location on the front of the cab cowl. On previous trucks the brake master cylinder had been located under the floorboards, a very difficult position from which to check and fill the brake-fluid reservoir.

The A series remained in production through 1958. A brief, but sharp recession that coincided with the A line's production time-frame caused International's truck sales to drop to 81,213 units (all weight classes), the lowest sales number in International's post-war history. Industry wide, truck production fell by 20 percent, a 20-year low. However, because of International's strong sales position in previous years, 10.8 percent of all trucks on the road carried the familiar Triple Diamond or IH insignias.

1959 B Series

The most easily recognized features of the revised B-line styling are a grid pattern egg-crate style grille and quad headlights set vertically in pairs. The biggest "news" of the new series was not styling, but the availability of V-8 engines and a redesigned wide pickup box called the "bonus load." The V-8 engines came in three sizes, with 266, 304, and 345 cubic-inch displacements. Only the 266 was available in International's light-duty truck models, the 304 and 345 being slated for the larger medium and heavy-duty trucks. In the light-duty range, the standard engines remained sixes. The B-100 models came standard with the 220 Black Diamond engine, while B-110- and B-120-series trucks came with the 240 BD. The stronger 264 BD six engine could be special-ordered for B-110, 120, 130 truck models, but the 266 V-8 was available across the light-duty range.

For the B series, International designed a true wide box, offered in 7 and 8 1/2-foot lengths. These "Bonus Load" boxes were available on all light-duty models, B-100 through B-130. The name "Bonus Load" came from the smooth-sided box's expanded interior width. Since the tailgate was narrower than the box's interior (caused by thick rear corner supports) items wider than four feet would not fit through the tailgate opening.

Mechanically, a higher speed 3.73 rear axle ratio replaced the 4.10 gearing, which had been standard on S- and A-series 1/2-ton trucks. Even with 6.50-16 tires, the 4.10 rear end gearing had caused excessive engine wear. An even higher 3.54 rear axle accompanied the automatic transmission.

International carried over its B-series trucks into 1960 with only one major change. The V-266 was made standard. The 240 Black Diamond

A-line trucks benefited from a completely redesigned cab that sat lower to the ground, eliminating running boards. The new cabs offered improved ventilation, more comfortable seating, and that most important 1950s styling feature—the wrap-around windshield.

six could still be ordered for its light-duty trucks, but to get the six, buyers had to delete the V-8 from the order form. External appearance changes were limited to a silver background on the front hood emblem (for 1959 this emblem's background had been black) and V emblems on the sides of the front fenders behind the headlights for trucks with V-8 engines.

Although sales of B-series trucks regained much of the ground lost in the 1958 recession, trucks from this styling series are very rarely seen today.

chapter ten

1961-1968 TRUCKS:
The Series Alphabet Repeats Itself

International introduced its new C-series trucks on November 1, 1960, as 1961 models. Although the cab and box stampings were carried over from the previous B series an appearance of new styling was achieved by reworking the cab mountings so that the cab sat lower on the frame. Rather than the body perching on top of the frame, as had been the case in previous years, the lower portion of the doors and rocker panels now hung down past the frame channels. Hot rodders call this technique "channeling" and it is done to retain most internal and external dimensions while dropping overall body height. In International's case, the only structural change inside the cab was a higher transmission hump, which did present somewhat of a leg room problem for anyone of lanky proportions who might occupy the center of the seat.

With its 1963 and 1964 C-series trucks, International added an "0" to the model number, making this truck, which is owned by George Mitchell, a C-1300 model.

Clearest evidence of the lowered cab comes from a side-view. On a B-series pickup, the top of the box levels squarely with the door handles. On the new C series, the top of the box leveled nearly with the window ledges. On the wide Bonus Load box, the beltline crease now lined up with the styling crease that cut across the door from the crest of the front fenders and edge of the hood, which gives one to think that the Bonus Load box had been designed with the lowered cab in mind. A lower, wider grille with horizontally grouped quad headlights further emphasized the C series' lower profile.

A bright metal grille and headlight rims gave even stripped-down, no-frills trucks a dressed up look. However, both bright metal pieces were stamped from easily dented anodized aluminum. Inside, however, International dressed its C-series trucks in subdued colors, soil-resistant charcoal for the upholstery and light tan on the dash. All other interior metal surfaces were painted body color.

Increased attention to comfort and convenience led to a more efficient heater, a foot-operated emergency brake lever replacing the former handle type, and two-speed electric windshield wipers. Two-speed wipers may not seem like a big improvement, but it takes only about five minutes of driving in a rain storm to appreciate the consistent operation of electric wipers over the erratic, hesitating action of vacuum-powered wipers. As a safety improvement, International's light-duty trucks were now fitted with a fuse block located under the dash on the left side. On previous light-duty models a fuse block had been nonexistent.

On the 1/2-ton C-100 pickup and Travelall models, International introduced a torsion-bar independent front suspension. Finally, owners and operators of International light-duty trucks could enjoy riding comfort approaching that of a car. Unlike General Motors, which abandoned torsion-bar front suspension on both its Chevrolet and GMC truck lines after just two years

International introduced its C-series trucks on November 1, 1960, as 1961 models. Four-wheel drive is a highly sought-after feature on 1960s vintage International trucks. The 1964 C 1200 four-wheel-drive model shown here is owned by Jack Lester.

(1960–1962) because of expense, International continued to equip its short wheelbase light-duty 100 (later called 1000) models with torsion-bar front suspension through 1974. Oddly, the C-110 pickup models also built on the 119-inch chassis used leaf springs and solid front axles.

International continued to build its 1/2-ton models on two wheelbases, both of which were longer in the C series. As noted, the short wheelbase now measured 119 inches (5 inches longer than previously). The long box 1/2-ton also added 5 inches to its wheelbase, for an axle-to-axle length of 131 inches. Trucks with the longer wheelbases used two-piece driveshafts with a center carrier bearing.

Light-duty C models could be ordered with a variety of six-cylinder and V-8 engines. Following the procedure established in the B series, buyers got the V-266 V-8 engine as standard equipment and had to special order a six. Available engines included the BD (Black Diamond) 220 and 240 sixes or the V-266 and V-304 eights. Both the BD-240 six and 304 V-8 engines could be modified to burn LPG fuel. A three-speed and overdrive man-

ual transmission was added to the range of gear-box offerings, which included the standard-equipment manual three-speed, a manual four-speed, and Borg Warner three-speed automatic.

C Series Travelall and Panel Models

Like the pickups, the basic Travelall/panel truck body shell, although unchanged, sat lower on the frame, giving the appearance of reworked styling. On Travelalls the most significant change was the addition of a second door on the driver's side. Having rear doors on both sides of the truck allowed rear seat passengers to enter or exit the vehicle with much greater convenience than had been the case on earlier models that had the single rear door on the passenger side.

Travelalls in both the C-100 C-110 models could be optioned with a custom package that included a flip-down tailgate and electric roll-up rear window, plus chrome body moldings. The C-110 Travelall was fitted with side-hinged rear doors as standard equipment. Depending on the vehicle's intended use, buyers could outfit a Travelall with either two or three seats. When a

Although International trucks generally have a strong reputation for reliability, the engines and drivetrains of the 1961–1968 models were particularly rugged. Powered by a 304 V-8, the 1965 D-1100-series 4x4 pickup shown here has clocked over a quarter-million miles with no major repairs. Todd Flaaten, its owner, reports, "The motor still runs strong and doesn't burn oil—just leaks a little."

third seat was installed, the second seat had a folding section on the passenger side for access to the rear.

Panel delivery models used the same body stampings as the Travelall with the rear quarter windows blanked in. Although other panel delivery manufacturers were flooring the cargo area with plywood or metal, International continued to build the cargo floor from wooden planks and skid strips. It's debatable whether wooden planks made a superior flooring material, but they certainly were more labor-intensive to install—another sign that International didn't build to price.

The C series continued through 1962 visibly unchanged, although a few very minor mechanical changes can be noted, such as a revised generator mounting bracket, designed to eliminate the idler pulley.

1962–1964 C Series

That fact that International was using six-year-old body shells remained well camouflaged by the lower body profile, but to keep in step with the competition in 1963 the C line received

Although the gauge cluster design of International trucks lacks the styling razz-matazz found on a Ford or Chevrolet, it does contain full instrumentation in easy-to-read round gauges.

The Travelall in this scene is climbing the summit road on Mt. Washington, the highest peak in the Northeastern United States. Companies transporting sightseers to the top of Mt. Washington and other such attractions often operated fleets of Internationals, selected for the built-in ruggedness of IH vehicles.

a new grille and single headlights. Quad headlights, which had been introduced in 1958 with much fanfare and promoted as a safety lighting feature, were now considered an outdated styling mark—hence the return to single headlights. Attention had now turned to the parking lights, where amber was considered a better safety attracter than white.

It seems that the trucks' badges underwent the biggest changes. For 1963, a simple IH badge replaced the former winged hood emblem. Number badges on the front fenders told the new model designation scheme which added a 0 to the model number used formerly, as in C-1000, C-1100, etc. Trucks with V-8 engines had a V under this model badge. Apparently believing the trucks' identity to be unmistakably established, International removed its nameplates from the sides of the hood.

By adding some plumbing and a PCV valve, International's engineers took a small step toward reducing vehicular air pollution. Of more immediate significance, they replaced the generator, a rather inefficient charging device, with the technologically superior alternator, which had been developed by Chrysler Corporation. At some point in mid-1964, cables replaced chains as the tailgate supports.

C-900 Compact Pickup

In the early 1960s as an offshoot of the compact car phenomenon, each of the major US truck producers introduced a compact pickup. The reasoning behind this short-lived compact pickup craze is a little hard to understand. The VW Kombi, Volkswagen's pickup model, had enjoyed strong U.S. sales in the later 1950s, but VW's penetration of the U.S. light-duty truck market had been blunted by the so-called "Chicken Tax," a heavy import fee imposed by the Kennedy administration specifically against West German-built light-duty trucks. Nonetheless, Ford, Chevrolet, and Dodge had all developed downsized, fuel-frugal pickups, and International apparently thought it, too, should join the fray. However, rather than actually developing an all-new model, International took its narrow-box,

1/2-ton pickup, shortened the wheelbase to 107 inches, cut back the box length to 6 feet, replaced the standard V-8 with the four-cylinder Scout engine, and created a light-duty truck specifically engineered for economy.

Called the C-900, International's economy pickup was highly maneuverable and attractively, if not expensively, appointed (the doors had vinyl coverings and the seat cushion featured a striped insert). However, the standard 4.09:1 rear axle ratio caused the 93-horsepower, 152-ci engine to work in its upper rpm range at highway speeds, leading to premature engine wear and giving the driver the impression that the engine was going to self-destruct if pushed past legal speed limits. The low gearing had been required to enable the under-powered engine to pull the truck's 3,250 pounds (unloaded) weight. According to a road test published in *Car Life* magazine, fuel consumption for the C-900 ranged between 16 to 20 miles per gallon, numbers that seem to stretch the truck's "economy" claim. Another problem, the C-900's short wheelbase and stiff suspension (torsion bar's weren't used on this economy model), caused the truck to bound like a pogo stick over rough roads.

With the introduction of the D series in 1965, International's economy pickup became the D-900 and was made available with a shortened version of the wide pickup box. In 1966 it was called the 900-A. For 1967 the 900 pickup abandoned its masquerade as an economy model. Now called the 908-B, the 226-ci V-8 became standard and a longer 115-inch wheelbase model was made available. With little besides base price as a purchasing incentive, the so-called "economy" 900 model pickup disappeared from International's model listings in 1969.

1965 D Series

The D line that appeared in the winter of 1964–1965 wore a new grille with vertical slots. Spin-on oil filters, now used on both the 6 and V-8, represented the most noticeable mechanical change. Optional custom cab models now featured richer-looking padded door panels and interior trim.

1966 A Series

It takes a trained eye to distinguish between a 1965 and 1966 International light-duty truck, and yet the 1966 models adopted a new series designation. The most noticeable external difference between a 1965 D-line model and a 1966 A-series truck is the bar extending across the center of the

Newest ways to answer the call of the wild

The very newest ways to hit the trail are with the great INTERNATIONAL® campermobiles.

Rough, tough, powerful INTERNATIONAL pickups—with two or four-door styling and fancy interiors—will carry your camper just about anywhere you want to go.

You can get a husky chassis with 131-in. wheelbase—and slide a fully-equipped camper into a new 8-ft. Bonus-Load body. Or you can get an extra-strong chassis with a long 140-in. wheelbase—and fit a roomier full-mount camper on it.

If you don't need all that room or power, try our SCOUT® camper. With all-wheel drive, it'll go way back in where the fishing is really good. And you can get it with custom interior and comfortable bucket seats.

Then there's our TRAVELALL®

International Harvester Company
Dept. PM-4, P. O. Box 7333
Chicago, Illinois 60601

Please send me your Camper Catalog.

Name

Address

City   State

wagon, which you can see at any INTERNATIONAL Dealer. A big, family wagon—available in two or four-wheel drive—it carries nine people plus their gear. And it hauls a house trailer without wagging its tail.

For anything else you want to know about our great line of recreational vehicles, see an INTERNATIONAL Dealer. Or fill in the coupon and mail it to us. We'll send you free a big, handsome catalog on our pickups, SCOUT and TRAVELALL.

INTERNATIONAL HARVESTER COMPANY
CHICAGO, ILLINOIS

International responded to the pickup camper craze that swept American society in the 1960s with specially designed "campermobile" models. Here again International relied on its reputation for proven reliability to attract buyers.

Now! The lowest-priced V-8 pickup you can buy.

Meet the new high-styled 908B

—the lowest priced V-8 pickup truck* in the field. Only the INTERNATIONAL* 908B gives you big V-8 value in a standard size pickup at this money-saving price.

All the famous INTERNATIONAL features are standard: rugged, truck-styled chassis, heavy gauge body, stronger suspension, plus full safety package including new, easier steering. You get INTERNATIONAL's extra comfort, too, in the 908B, with the smart 1967 styling that sets the pace in the pickup field.

Why pay more for a full-powered V-8 when you can get it in the world's finest pickup for less? Test drive the new 908B at your nearest INTERNATIONAL Dealer. He can save you more all the way, and he's ready to deliver. International Harvester Company, Chicago, Illinois 60611.

IH. INTERNATIONAL® TRUCKS

*Based on manufacturer's list prices for comparably equipped V-8 models, including heater and defroster. Add state and local taxes, destination and handling charges.

In an attempt to compete with Ford, GM, and Chrysler in the compact pickup market, International developed its 900-series light-duty trucks. Essentially a built-to-price short-box pickup, the original 900 model featured the Scout's 4 cylinder engine, which proved underpowered in the heavier pickup truck. With the 908B model, offered in 1967, International combined V-8 power with budget pricing.

Owners praise the ruggedness of International's four-wheel-drive mechanism. A testimony to this is the widespread use of 4wd International trucks by the U.S. military during the 1960s.

grille carrying the International name. On trucks with painted bumpers the color now was white. Custom cab pickups featured a wood grain dash and on all pickup models, standard or custom, a new perforated three-piece headliner replaced the former two-piece headliner with its center retaining strip.

1967 B Series

Of the numerous changes marking the 1967 B line, the revised grille is probably the most apparent. In contrast to the "toothy" grille of previous years, the new grille consisted of a rectangular section of black mesh set in a bright metal frame. A wider International nameplate stretched across the mesh material in the center of the grille. The change to a shorter 8-foot Bonus Load box isn't so noticeable unless a truck with the earlier 8 1/2-foot Bonus Load box is parked alongside. The 8-foot box may have been a mid-year change as both the 8 1/2 and 8-foot Bonus Load boxes are listed in the 1967 specification sheets.

Among the mechanical changes were federally mandated safety features, including a fail-safe braking system using a dual master cylinder and brake fluid warning light. Larger brake shoes and drums increased braking effectiveness. Four-way flashers were made standard equipment and door locks were of the safety type. An electrically operated windshield washer replaced the previous push-bulb type and was made standard equipment.

1968 C Series

For the second time in a decade, International used the C-series designation. However, only very minor changes marked the 1968 C line of light-duty trucks. The most noticeable change is the absence of the IH emblem from the front of the hood. A smaller version of this emblem now appeared on the front fenders behind the wheel openings where the model badge had been. The optional chrome side spears on bonus load trucks now extended the full length of the vehicle and a second decorative bright-metal strip was applied to the rocker panels, giving a more dressed-up appearance. In accordance with federal safety regulations, side marker lights were added to the front fenders.

From 1961 to 1968, sales of International light-duty trucks (under 6,000 pounds GVW) held steady at slightly over 48,000 units annually. However, light truck sales by other manufacturers were skyrocketing. In 1965, the combined light-duty truck sales of Chevrolet and Ford reached nearly one million. By comparison, International wasn't just losing ground, it was in danger of being lost in the dust. To stay in the light truck business, it was time for International to catch up—and doing so meant all new styling and an image expansion that would bring in buyers who had not previously owned an International (something the Scout had done with great success). This was the mission of International's all-new D-line full-size pickups, panels, and Travelalls that appeared in November 1968.

chapter eleven

1969-1975 TRUCKS:
Pickups and Travelalls with a Scout Look

The new look of International's light-duty trucks came from the drawing boards of the talented designer Ted Ornas and, not surprisingly, the result reflected a clear family tie with the Scout—Ornas's most notable design success. From the simple, almost flat grille to the angular body lines and rectangular window outlines, there was no mistaking the manufacturer of International's new trucks—it had to be the same outfit that built the Scout. Although the new styling had a no-nonsense, functional look about it, the squared-off lines were also up-to-date. Ford's new truck line, introduced in 1967, had an equally crisp, utilitarian look. And Ford's light trucks were selling like lotto tickets the eve before the $10 million drawing. Unfortunately, International's new light-duty truck models were not a sales success. Production of light-duty trucks for 1969 (not including Scout) came to only 41,174. This is pretty dismal, not only in comparison with Ford's 639,948 light-duty trucks built during the same period and Chevrolet's light truck production of 643,622 (remember that for years International held third place in light-duty truck sales), but also because the 41,174 sales figure represented a loss of almost 4,000 units from 1968. What was going wrong?

The sales problem certainly had no connection with the design or engineering of International's trucks, which were in many ways the best the company had ever built.

Something else had to be keeping buyers away. Keith Mazurek, who served as President of the Truck Group at International during the mid-1970s, states that one of the reasons buyers bypassed the company's new-look trucks is that many first-time truck owners bought their new truck from the dealerships where they had formerly purchased cars. Since International truck dealerships were not located in high-traffic areas (most were placed where they could best serve farmers and contractors), many buyers had not only never set foot in an International dealership, they had never even drove past one. To combat this lack of product visibility, International embarked on a program to sign up dealers carrying car franchises. Keep in mind that during this period many dealerships sold only one make of car and unless they had a Chevy, Dodge, or Ford franchise, most likely did not carry a truck line. It was these dealers that International wanted to link up with, particularly to expand outlets for the Scout, but also to increase sales of its light-duty trucks. There may have been a little wishful thinking here, but these are the projections that International management made in the mid-1970s for the prospects of expanding the sales network—principally through offering Scout and light-duty truck franchises to car dealerships.

International's 1969–1975 light truck lineup consisted of an impressive array of models that included two- and four-wheel-drive pickups, Travelalls, and Travelettes (crew cab pickups), plus the Scout.

In designing International's new D models, IHC stylist Ted Ornas gave light trucks a clear family resemblance with the Scout. The Bonus Load pickup box, as seen on this truck, underwent complete restyling to blend the box with the new cab and front end treatment. Whereas the side stampings for International's earlier wide boxes are single sheets of metal, the Bonus Load boxes from 1969 to 1975 have double side walls—a construction that prevents object thrown against the inner box wall from denting the outer panel. The truck shown here is a 1972 model, originally purchased for fire department use, now owned by Robert Piland, who reports that the Warn winch was a very rare factory accessory.

Projected IH Dealer Network

	1979	1981	1983	1985
IH dealers	1,650	1,750	1,850	1,900
Auto/IH dealers	450	850	1,050	1,200

Note that while traditional IH dealers, those that also sold medium and heavy-duty trucks as well as farm equipment, were expected to increase during the projected half-decade (ironically the projections are for the period immediately after IH ceased produc- tion of light trucks, including Scout), the growth of exclusive IH dealers is small compared to the three-fold growth projected for the auto/IH dealer network.

The feasibility of a strong auto dealer/IH network never had a chance to be tested as International ceased production of its light trucks in 1975 and production of Scouts in 1980. It might have worked, but International was experiencing other problems besides sales, which we will discuss later. Let's turn to brighter things and examine the new-look light-duty truck models.

International unveiled its completely reworked light trucks, called the D models, in November 1968. (Although the cab was new to pickup buyers, it had appeared a year earlier on International's Fleetstar medium heavy-duty trucks.) Of International's new pickups and Travelalls, the ad copy boasted, "They are new in 83 different ways. So this is obviously not just a routine model change. New in engineering, styling, and comfort." Indeed, the changes were more than skin deep. A cross-flow radiator gave increased cooling capacity. A printed circuit board with plug-in connectors for the instruments helped assure more trouble-free operation (through from a restorer's point-of-view printed circuit boards can be a nightmare, because if they fail, they're almost impossible to repair), while in-tank fuel filters helped prevent gas line and carburetor plugging. Wider shoes and brake drums front and rear on 1000 through 1300 models assured improved stopping power; the 1500 models featured wider as well as larger diameter front brakes.

The list of improvements goes on. A new double-jointed steering column, attached to a Saginaw recirculating ball steering box that replaced the former Gemmer worm and roller steering mechanism, soaked up steering vibrations. Recirculating ball steering, a design that originated at GM in the early 1940s, required much less steering effort. Refinements included beefed-up bumpers, as well as heavier wheels and tie-rod ends. The sales literature also described as improvements unitized cab construction, panel joints sealed with a thermo-setting plastic, doors and windows "that fit like a glove," improved springing that "smooths out humps and bumps," new body mounts that "actually divorce the body from the frame to all but eliminate road vibrations," and an exhaust system that "deadens noise and vibration more effectively than ever before." Indeed the 1969 D series and later International trucks do have a more solid feel and are better insulated and quieter than previous models.

Light trucks were being purchased for a greater variety of uses than ever before. By the mid to late 1960s, one of the most popular pickup applications was as a recreation vehicle, either being fitted with a slide-in camper unit or hauling a camper trailer. Accordingly, International expanded its option list for the new D series beyond that offered on any previous International light-duty truck. Deluxe interior appointments

could be optioned that included custom bucket seats with a lockable storage console in the center and a floor mat that extended under the seat for improved sound and temperature insulation. For comfort, the option list included air conditioning and a super-capacity heater with a three-speed blower. Optional power steering and power brakes made for easier driving and greater safety. A camper package, available for an extra cost of only $69, outfitted International's light trucks for the job of carrying a slide-in pickup camper. For distance travel, buyers could option an auxiliary gas tank. With fuel consumption of V-8-equipped trucks averaging about 10 miles per gallon, the auxiliary tank was a popular option. On Travelalls, the extra fuel tank sits behind the front wheelwell on the passenger side and the filler cap fits flush with the fender, as was the case with the main tank filler outlet on the 1961–1965 models. Switching between tanks is done by turning a knob on the instrument panel which not only diverts the fuel source, but also connects the fuel gauge to the sending unit in the tank now feeding the engine. A radio and eight-track tape player could be optioned to provide entertainment during those long distance drives. Other extras included a heavy-duty rear-step bumper and dress-up imitation woodgrain side trim, which extended from the rear of the front wheel opening to the end of the bonus load box.

Important as the engineering and comfort changes were, styling is what really set International's new trucks apart. As mentioned, the Scout imprint gave the light-duty models a functional boxy look, but the low silhouette also emphasized the truck's length and width. From a frontal view, however, the added width is quite deceptive because the grille, now set inside the leading edges of the front fenders, actually makes the D-series trucks look narrower than their predecessors. Even when styling changes are as radical as those seen on International's 1969 pickups and Travelalls, there is always a link with the earlier models to maintain continuity and preserve manufacturer identify. On the 1969 and 1970 light-duty Internationals, the grille bar with the International name, set inside a rectangular, black grille opening, and twin air inlets on the panel below the grille provide that link. Everything else about the trucks' styling is new. A mildly curved windshield replaced the swept back windshield of the 1957 through 1968 pickups and Travelalls. The rear window, which appears identical to that on earlier models, is actually somewhat deeper. The gas tank filler for the main tank is now in the more traditional pickup

Probably the rarest of all D-model pickups is the four-door, two-seat Travelette. The extremely long wheelbase made this model difficult to maneuver, but its crew-sized cab appealed to construction companies and other businesses that needed a truck capable of transporting work crews to the job site.

location at door handle height at the rear corner on the driver's side of the cab.

Inside, an elegantly simple three-spoke steering wheel harmonized with the functionally attractive instrument layout which now followed a horizontal pattern and nestled under a padded dash hood that extended the width of the cab. The arrangement of the instruments remained as before with the speedometer in the center flanked by gauges for fuel level, engine coolant temperature, oil pressure, and electrical system status. International's brochures emphasized the benefits of complete instrumentation to prospective buyers. Of course, gauges that actually monitor the engine's vital functions are far superior to so-called "idiot" warning lights that illuminate after a problem (such as low oil pressure) has already damaged the engine. A heater control panel with sliding knobs (similar to the heater control panel used on 1967–1972 Chevrolets) replaced the pull-out knobs used with some heaters installed on previous models.

The padded dash, as well as the seat upholstery, steering wheel and column, and other interior trim were all color-coordinated with the exterior. This was a first for International trucks. The coordinating interior colors consisted of blue,

green, red, or black. On trucks with a Custom interior, the floor mat also matched the interior color. Another sign of International's eye to detail, a boot surrounded the steering column where it enters the lower part of the instrument panel.

The consumer advocate movement of the 1960s had pushed vehicle safety to the forefront of public awareness with the result that federal legislation had mandated several safety features, including side-marker lights, fail-safe braking systems, and seat belts. International took the opportunity of its redesigned trucks to incorporate safety features beyond those required by the government. These included the deeply padded dash which, as mentioned earlier, now extended all the way across the cab, paddle-type (seatbelt latch style) interior door handles that fit into the now standard dual arm rests replacing of the previous lever-type handles, and restyled window cranks, which have a flatter profile—a safety feature as well as an appearance plus. Padded dual sun visors finally became standard equipment. To protect the driver from chest injuries in the event of a head-on crash, International now fitted its light-duty trucks with a collapsible steering column.

Not all changes were improvements. One of the least successful is the redesigned glove compartment which now became a bin fastened to the door rather than the familiar cardboard enclosure. Although the bin gives easy access to a few, neatly stored items easily available, it doesn't work very well for holding the collection of tools, papers, maps, spare fuses, and other odds and ends that truck owners typically throw into a glove box. The fuse block continued to be placed inside the glove box, making fuse replacement very easy. This fuse location was an IH exclusive at that time. Owners of 1969–1975 light-duty International trucks will be interested to know that the build sheet (a paper detailing the truck's original equipment) was attached to the back of the glove bin during assembly. By pushing the clips on the side of the bin, the tray can be flipped down to reveal a sheet listing the truck's original axle ratio, transmission, engine size, options and special equipment.

The wide bonus load pickup body had also received a restyling to blend smoothly with the new cab and front end sheet metal. International had been the last truck builder to use heavy-gauge metal in its pickup boxes, but with new stampings for the redesigned box came an opportunity to use thinner metal, so the wide boxes built from 1969 through 1975 have double side walls to prevent objects thrown against the inner wall from denting the outer panels. The higher window ledges on the new cabs allowed the sidewalls on the wide box also to be slightly higher—giving increased load space. A big improvement was a full-width tailgate. The thick rear pillars of the 1957–1968 wide box resulted in a tailgate only a little wider than that on a narrow box. The full-width tailgate made for easier loading of bulky items and the tailgate's lever-type latch (like that used by Chevrolet) enabled the operator to open the tailgate with one hand. Inside the box, wheel housings with a squared-off shape helped avoid the wasted space and difficulty in stacking items that occurs in pickups with rounded wheel housings.

The 1969–1975 narrow boxes are basically the same as those used previously, except that the lengths are shortened to 6 1/2 (swb) and 8 feet (lwb). If the spare tire is mounted in the optional location under the rear of the box, the rear fenders on 1969–1974 narrow box pickups (a narrow box was not offered in 1975) carry the same part numbers as those on earlier trucks. If a side-mounted spare is installed, it is on the left side. The tailgate also has the same part number as the previous models, but the 1969–1975 parts book lists a cable in place of the tailgate chain shown for 1961–1965. The covered cable is superior to the chain, which rattles around and soon wears

the rubber protector off and then bangs against the box and scratches the paint.

In the early years, International had outsourced the engines used in its light trucks. The purchase of production rights to the Willys six in the early 1930s gave the company's light trucks an International engine. With the completion in 1939 of the Indianapolis engine plant, International greatly increased its ability to provide its own engines, not only for the light-duty, but also for its heavier duty trucks. International's exclusive use of its own engines in light-duty truck models came to an end in 1969 with the adoption of the AMC-built 232-ci, 145-horsepower six as the base engine in the light-duty 1/2-ton 1010D model. This AMC engine had an oversquare design which meant that the bore was larger than the stroke. International's Black Diamond sixes had been under-square (longer stroke than bore). Short-stoke (under-square) engines typically generate their power at higher rpms, which is beneficial for lighter-weight vehicles like cars, whose power requirements come at higher speeds. Trucks, however, need power at low rpms, and long-stroke (under-square) engines typically produce their power at low speeds. From this perspective, adoption of the AMC engine would seem not to have been in the best interest of buyers of the new line of International light trucks. But there were reasons. International could purchase the AMC 232 six for less than the company could build its BD sixes, and cost was becoming a critical factor in International's ability to field products at competitive prices. Also with light trucks serving more and more as everyday transport, usually unloaded, there was less and less need for an engine that produced its power at low speeds. In its favor, too, the AMC six weighed about 170 pounds less than the engine it replaced. Then there was a design advantage in that the AMC engine featured seven main bearings while the older IH sixes had four main bearings. The greater number of main bearings meant better crankshaft support, leading to longer engine life. Heavier duty 1/2-ton 1110D and 4x4 models still came equipped with the BD-241 engine. The 1210D models came standard-equipped with the V-266 V-8, while the BG-265 six and V-304, V-345, and V-392 V-8s were available at extra cost.

Buyers of International light trucks could pick from a greater selection of transmissions than could be found on the order forms of any other manufacturer. Besides the standard three-speed and four-speed, International made available a heavy-duty three-speed with floor shift, a Borg Warner three-speed

The Travelall shared the pickup's forward sheet metal, grille, front fenders, and hood. From the windshield back, however, the Travelall looked more like a car than a truck. With truck-type vehicles being used in settings other than the farm or construction site, two-tone paint schemes and dress-up trim that included chrome bumpers and bright metal trim were a popular option. This end-of-the-line 1975 Travelall is owned by Emil Tulenko.

automatic, and two five-speeds—one of which (the T-34) used fourth gear as direct drive and had an overdrive ratio in fifth. The five speeds gave great gearing flexibility, allowing a truck so equipped to run at optimum engine rpms through nearly any driving condition. The four and five-

speed transmissions had very low first gears that are useful in pulling trailers or operating off-road. The five-speed with overdrive is a desirable transmission for fuel economy and for reducing engine wear.

Rear axle ratios ranged from a fuel-saving 3.07:1 to a stump-pulling 4.56. Two optional

In 1971 the International nameplate was reduced in size and moved to a new location in the lower left corner of the grille, similar to its location on 1969–1970 Scouts. The headlights were brought into the grille also. With minor modifications, this basic grille layout continued through 1975.

heavy-duty rear axles were offered in the 1/2-ton 1000 and 1100 series. The anti-slip Powr-Lok feature was available at extra cost on both the standard-duty and heavy-duty rear axles. All International pickups and Travelalls, except the 1000-series models, could be equipped with auxiliary rear leaf springs.

The new D-line light-duty trucks came in four model series: the light-duty 1/2-ton 1000D; the heavier duty 1/2-ton 1010D; the 3/4-ton 1210D; and the 1-ton 1310D. Four-wheel drive was available in the 1010, 1210, and 1310 series. International continued to build its pickups in short and long wheelbase versions. Unlike previous years, in which wheelbase lengths varied from one load rating to the next, for International trucks built between 1969 and 1975, the 1000, 1010, and 1210 short-wheelbase pickups with the 6 1/2-foot box all used the same 115-inch wheelbase. Longer 8-foot box pickups used a 131-inch wheelbase. The light-duty 1000 models continued to feature the torsion bar independent front suspension, while the heavier duty 1010, 1210, and 1310 models used a beam front axle. Frame construction also differed between the 1000 and

1010 and higher models, with the 1000 having a box-type frame, while the 1010 and up had channel-style frames.

Besides two-wheel or four-wheel drive and short or long wheelbase, buyers of International pickups could also select either the traditional single-seat cab or the two-seat Travelette. Either could be ordered without a pickup box for fitting with a platform or other special body. International also continued to build the Travelall through the end of its light truck production in 1975.

Travelall

Like the pickup, the Travelall had also been completely restyled and given a strong family resemblance with the Scout. As would be expected, the Travelall shared the pickup's forward sheet metal (grille, front fenders, and hood). From the windshield back, however, the Travelall looked more like a car than a truck. Interior finishings were also more car-like than any previous International model. The vinyl seat coverings had weave inserts and a cover was provided for the spare tire. Realizing that most buyers used their Travelalls as heavy-duty station wagons,

Asked whether International built any special model light trucks, most truck historians (and readers of this book) would answer "yes, the 1957 Golden Anniversary Special." Of course that answer would be correct, but even most serious truck enthusiasts aren't aware that International marketed another special model, called the "Johnny Reb," in the southeastern states only in 1971. This truck is instantly recognized by its orange color and two white stripes, each with three red stars, running down the hood. Why a special model offered only to International truck buyers in "Dixie?" The southeast has long been strong International truck country and with the "Johnny Reb" special IH might grab sales from Ford and Chevrolet. Even in the 1970s, in the south and west a young man's first "car" was likely to be a truck—and what an impression a young blade would make driving down Main Street in an orange "Johnny Reb" International pickup— especially one fitted with the 392 engine.

International fitted these versatile carriers with tailgates as standard equipment and made panel-style rear doors an option. On a standard model, the operator lowered or raised the rear window with a hand crank, but an electrically operated window was available as an option.

In standard form, Travelalls came fitted with a single bench seat like a pickup. Few were delivered like this. Most have both front and second seats. The second seat, which is accessed through the rear side doors, folds down flush with the floor. This is a beneficial design because it gives a flat load space. In earlier Travelalls, this second seat folded against the back of the front seat— taking away some of the load space. An optional third seat gave the Travelall a nine-passenger (including driver) seating capacity. As International's ads pointed out, the Travelall offered a comfort advantage over nine-passenger station wagons due to chair-height seating and full shoulder and head room on all three seats. Another advantage over a nine-passenger station wagon, the rear seat of the Travelall faced forward and passengers entered the third seat through the side doors (part of the second seat folded down), as opposed to entering the rear-facing seat found in most station wagons by climbing through the tailgate opening. Because the third seat took up most of the luggage space, Travelalls could be fitted with an optional roof-mounted luggage rack.

Although the Travelall retained the 119-inch wheelbase of previous models, it shared the chassis (other than wheelbase length) and suspension design with the same series long-box pickups. Travelalls in the 1000 series featured the smooth-riding torsion bar front suspension while the 1100 and 1200 models had straight front axles with leaf springs. Like pickups, Travelalls could also be fitted with four-wheel drive. Due to clearance for the front drive axle and stiffer springs, an unmodified four-wheel-drive Travelall sits about three inches higher than a two-wheel-drive version. Four-wheel-drive Travelalls have a much harsher ride due to their stiffer springing and are not recommended for strictly highway use. But for pulling a heavy trailer or off-road driving, a 4x4 Travelall can't be beat.

While painted bumpers were standard, a trim package that included chrome bumpers and bright metal windshield trim, as well as bright headlight and parking light bezels and rocker trim was a popular option. Travelalls were also offered with the woodgrain side trim that could also be optioned on pickups. Chrome hubcaps and full-wheel covers added to the dress-up look. Painted hub caps were standard. Due to the popularity of travel trailers, Travelalls could be fitted with class III or class IV hitches at the factory.

Panel bodies based on the Travelall continued to be available, but because of the increasing popularity of vans, traditional panel trucks based on 1/2-ton pickup chassis were now practically extinct.

1970–1975 Trucks

Through the remaining six years of International light truck production, only minor changes occurred and these are most visible in

Designed for use in medium-duty trucks and power plants for a variety of agricultural and industrial machines, International's V-8 engines have near legendary ruggedness and reliability. In 1975, International equipped all its engines with electronic ignition, a change that substantially reduced tune-up maintenance.

three variations to the grille styling. The 1970 light-duty trucks carried over the 1969 grille with its center bar. For 1971 the bar was deleted, the area of the grille surrounding the headlights was painted black, and an International nameplate was affixed to the grille inset on the left-hand (driver's) side, the same location as the IH insignia on the Scout grille. The model years 1972 through 1975 saw barred grilles of two different designs. The 1972 and 1973 grille featured horizontal bars with a center divider, while on the 1974 and 1975 pickups and Travelalls, the grille consisted of horizontal bars running the full length between the headlights. In 1971, International abandoned its policy of upgrading its trucks at any point during the calendar year and followed the rest of the industry in making changes only at new model introductions. According to the statement that

announced the annual model change policy, the reason for waiting until new model time to make upgrades wasn't a response to pressure from the competition, but a need to make government mandated safety and emissions upgrades on a scheduled basis. While this statement may reflect basic truth, pressure to offer the public what appeared to be new trucks on an annual basis was certainly there.

Annual model changes notwithstanding, from 1969 on, any updating of IH's light-duty trucks was barely visible. Besides the different grille, the 1971 models also sported optional rocker panel trim similar to that found on Chevy's upclass Cheyenne pickups, model designation badges on the front fenders, and restyled deluxe full hubcaps. The new barred grille marked the "big" change for 1972. To tell a 1973

The angular emphasis, so noticeable on the exterior, carried over on the interior where a horizontally shaped instrument panel housed a full complement of gauges.

IH pickup or Travelall from a 1972, you'll probably have to look at the emblems on the sides of the front fenders, which are rectangular in shape and positioned higher above the side-marker lights in 1973. Changes for 1974 consisted of a new grille without the center bar and revised model designations. The 1/2-tons now became the 100 series and the 3/4-tons the 200 series. In the Travelall and 100-series 4x4 pickup, the 345-ci V-8 became the standard engine.

Oddly, the final year for International's pickups and Travelalls saw more changes than any of the previous six years of this styling package. Most significant, the base model became the 150, reflecting an increase in load capacity to avoid

new Federal exhaust emission requirements (that included catalytic converters) for trucks under 6,000 GVW. International engineers boosted the 150's load capacity simply by installing the 1974 model 100's HD front coil springs along with six-leaf rear springs and fitting larger H78-15 tires. Ford applied a similar upgrade to its F-100, creating the popular F-150 in much the same manner and for the same reason that International created its 150 series. The difference in the two companies' approaches is that Ford continued to build the standard 1/2-ton F-100, while IH dropped its 100 models. Also dropped were the less popular Travelall-based Travelette, the five-speed transmission, and the narrow pickup box.

Patrick Lind shows his "daily driver" 1200-series 1970 International pickup with pride.

For its final year, International also switched its light trucks to electronic ignition. The higher energy electronic ignition gives much greater spark plug life, better starting, and a longer interval between tune-ups. New options included an auxiliary light package consisting of an under-hood light, map light, glove box light, and cargo light on the back of the cab on pickups and over the rear passenger or cargo area on the Travelall and a dealer-installed slide-in tool box. Canadian and U.S. 1969 and later International light trucks are nearly identical as all production now occurred in the the U.S. The main difference was the availability of the 266 V-8 in trucks sold in the United States.

International Gives Up Its Light Trucks

For the 1975 model year sales of IH pickups dropped to a ghostly 6,329 units, but this dismal figure is not the reason for the demise of International's light truck line. Rather, it reflects the decision by International management to get out of the light truck business. Pickup production for 1974 had totaled 36,584. While International completely missed the explosion in pickup sales that began in the mid-1960s, it can be argued from hindsight that a different marketing policy might have turned that around. As an example, International's ads almost completely ignored women. If a woman is displayed in an ad, she is in a passive role, riding in a truck with a man or looking at a truck. By the 1970s most manufacturers realized that large number of the vehicle purchasing decisions were being made by women.

International claimed that its light-duty trucks cost more to build than the competition's, in part because the low volume raised IH's per-truck share of new model tooling expense, and also because IH light-duty trucks shared the expensive-to-build heavy-duty engines with the medium-duty truck line. These explanations for a lower profit margin from the light-duty truck line may be true, but IH also added to its profitability problems by listing engine and transmission options on its pickups and Travelalls that better fitted a powertrain list for its medium-truck line. No other light-truck builder of the time offered buyers a five-speed transmission, nor International's engine choices.

Although corporate management takes a long look at the accountant's bottom line, sales and production costs weren't the real reason for International's killing its light-duty trucks. The actual explanation lies in corporate politics which pitched the big-truck guys against the little-truck guys. In a free-for-all scramble for product development capital, the big-truck guys won out. Of course, International dealerships played in this game, too, pushing sales of big trucks where they stood to make more money over the light-duty models. And so International killed its superbly engineered, well styled light trucks—though to its credit, the company retained and expanded its Scout offerings.

chapter twelve

THE SCOUT:
Trailblazing New Markets

Naming a new vehicle is a black art. When the name fits, it gives the vehicle instant identity. When the name doesn't fit, the vehicle becomes a hardly noticed piece of colored sheet metal. The Scout name worked; in fact it made a perfect descriptor for International's little truck/Travelall. Just think of the images the word "Scout" brings to mind: fearless warriors sneaking behind enemy lines, faithful guides and interpreters like those Native Americans who accompanied Lewis and Clark on their exploration of the Louisiana Purchase. The qualities that images like these present: adventurous, sure-footed, dependable, resourceful, also fit well the nimble 4x4 that International introduced in 1960 as the first serious challenger to the Jeep.

International's management didn't pick the Scout name from entries submitted to a contest or a list compiled by a committee. The name came about in a much more spontaneous way, as the nickname applied to the project assigned Ted Ornas, chief stylist for International's light-duty line, and his team of engineers. When the prototype was presented to management for production approval, the name also met with favor, but a trademark search revealed that a vehicle with the same name was being built in Canada. So International purchased the rights to the name, clearing the way for its use on the new vehicle.

Even as the Scout was fading into history, its designer, Ted Ornas, was trying to sell International management on a new-generation Scout that would use weight-saving composite body construction. This composite-based concept series was a decade ahead of its time and consequently only one prototype, a Sports Enthusiast model, code SSV, was built. This experimental Scout-of-the-future still exists and can be seen in the Auburn Museum in Auburn, Indiana.
John Glancy

Though essentially a short-wheelbase utility vehicle, the Scout was designed with multiple personalities fitting a wide range of uses. Purchased with the pickup cap, the Scout became a compact, economical-to-operate pickup truck. Covered with a full-length cap, the Scout became a mini-Travelall, capable of transporting up to six adults. Ordered without a top, the Scout became a fun-to-drive runabout. Fitted with four-wheel drive, which most were, the Scout was equally at home on or off-road. With two-wheel drive the Scout offered both economy of purchase and operation, as well as utility. In settings ranging from farms to fire departments, the Scout runabout served a multitude of uses.

Thanks to its highly versatile design, the Scout met instant success. Within a month of its introduction, Scout production doubled from 50 to 100 units a day. This increase required putting on a second shift for the first time in the Fort Wayne truck assembly plant's history. After another month, production was increased another 33 percent. By the end of the Scout's first calendar year, more than 35,000 copies had been sold, making it the hottest selling vehicle in International's history.

One of the reason's for its sales success, the Scout was a "helluva" buy. At a base price of $1,771 (for the 2wd version; 4wd listed at

One of the most unusual original-style Scouts is this dressed-up Aristocrat model. At a time when most buyers wanted a plain utilitarian vehicle, few Aristocrats were sold. *John Glancy*

$2,128.84 FOB Fort Wayne) the Scout undercut a Jeep's base price by $482. To keep development costs as low as possible, Ornas's engineering team had created the Scout's four-cylinder engine by cutting the left bank off International's 304 V-8. The resulting right-slanted four cylinder engine displaced 152 cubic inches and had a power rating of 93 horsepower. The 304 V-8 was a work horse engine for International's light and medium-duty trucks, and was used in industrial applications. The derivative Scout "Comanche" engine proved durable, and many internal parts, including the camshaft and crankshaft, interchanged, reducing manufacturing and parts inventory costs. As a further bonus, the slant-four proved quite economical to operate, getting 21–23 miles per gallon.

Although forecasts suggested that the majority of sales orders would be for two-wheel-drive pickups, the four-wheel-drive Travel Top version proved to be most popular: so popular, in fact, that nearly 80 percent of all Scouts were built as 4x4s. With its short wheelbase and four-wheel drive, the Scout was ideal for plowing snow. Many service stations bought Scouts for this use,

plus parts runs and road service. Rural mail carriers liked the Scout's sure-footed traction. Those who lived off the beaten path bought the Scout to ensure that they would get home in bad weather. Sportsmen were drawn to the Scout's off-road capability. Small contractors liked its ability to carry tools and supplies to the job site, and the list goes on. Simply stated, with the Scout International hit the jackpot on the first try.

Given the limitations of a very short wheelbase and functional, cheap-to-build boxy shape, Ted Ornas had given the Scout surprising good looks. The pickup looked better than the Travel-Top version, partly because the pickup box had a styling indent along the rear quarters that picked up the line from the rear of the pickup cap, but also because the Travel-Top emphasized the Scout's basic boxy shape. On the original Scout, the windshield folded flat against the hood. To allow this, the windshield wiper motors had to be mounted on

The Scout's success derived from its highly versatile design and easy conversion to pickup, station wagon style sport utility vehicle, or open runabout.

Which one's the Scout?

1

2

3

4

5

1 is. It's sporting the SCOUT vinyl cab top. (And that makes it a sporty pickup.) **2 is.** It's equipped with the SCOUT steel TRAVEL-TOP. (Just the thing for light delivery work around town. Or for traveling from town to town.) **3 is.** It's wearing the SCOUT steel cab top. (Recommended for winter duty north of the Mason-Dixon Line. So is a heater.) **4 is.** It's outfitted with the SCOUT vinyl TRAVEL-TOP. (Add bucket seats and an upholstered back seat and you have a jaunty little wagon.) **And 5 is,** too. Even though it doesn't have any kind of a top. And the windshield's folded forward. (Which means it's a SCOUT stripped down for fun.) Well, now that you know that each is a SCOUT—which one are you going to buy?

P.S. They all have a sturdy frame and rugged components and a 93 hp 4-cylinder engine that goes about 20 miles per gallon. Price is $1690.85.* See an INTERNATIONAL Dealer or Branch to test drive the SCOUT and buy it. International Harvester Co., 180 N. Michigan Ave., Chicago 1, Illinois.

THE
Scout ®
BY INTERNATIONAL®

At the end of 1975, as a result of the decision to cease production of the light truck line, International made available a stretched wheelbase Scout pickup called the Terra. With a cargo bed measuring a full 6-feet in length, the Terra offered the hauling capability of a short-box pickup, plus the traction of four-wheel drive.

the windshield header. A bracket in the center of the hood secured the windshield when it was lowered. To make the Scout easily convertible into a sporty runabout, both the top and doors were easily removable. The metal top could be lifted off by removing a few bolts, while the doors came off simply by lifting up on the hinges.

Early Scouts were fitted with a bench seat, another sign of International's forecasting predominant sales of two-wheel-drive models. Four-wheel drive's two shift levers (hi-lo range and in/out of 4wd), plus the standard shift selector all mounted on the transmission hump, left little foot room for the center passenger. The popularity of four-wheel drive would soon lead International to offer front bucket seats. In typical International fashion, the company introduced a steady stream of improvements, each making the Scout more civilized and better suited to highway driving.

In 1962, roll-up windows became optional (the early metal caps had been fitted with sliding side windows). A two-passenger rear seat was also added to the option list, as was a canvas top. The fabric top appealed to those who wanted to use their Scout as a sporting vehicle, but didn't want

to get wet when it rained. (The original runabout had been offered without a top.)

The major development for 1964 was the availability of turbocharging, a performance option that boosted the Scout's horsepower to 111 and the torque rating to 166 foot-pounds. (The maximum output figures for the normally aspirated engine remained 93 horsepower and 143 foot-pounds of torque.) With turbocharging a Scout's top speed was slightly over 80 miles per hour and acceleration improved to a quick 13.20 seconds for the 0–60-miles per hour sprint. The turbocharged four-cylinder engine remained a Scout option through 1967.

The first visual changes came in 1965, with the introduction of the Scout 800. The most noticeable changes were a fixed windshield with windshield wipers now located at the bottom of the windshield frame, and an International nameplate replacing the IH logo in the center of the grille. The fixed windshield eliminated irritating air drafts at the bottom of the windshield and didn't really detract from the Scout's sporting nature since as a matter of practicality few drivers drove around with the windshield in folded position.

To honor America's bicentennial, International offered two special trim models of the Scout called the "Spirit of '76" and the "Patriot." Essentially identical in appearance, both featured red and blue side trim on a Winter White body with the interior upholstered in Wedgwood Blue vinyl. With the "Spirit" package, buyers also got a blue denim fabric top, a sport steering wheel, roll bar, chrome wheels, and Goodyear "Tracker AT" 10 x 15 tires. *John Glancy*

Authentic "Spirit" Scouts are extremely rare as only 384 were manufactured. The "Spirit" package can be authenticated by the Spirit appliqué code number 10876 on the options list and "Spirit 76" hand written on the line setting ticket. *John Glancy*

To appeal to the off-roading crowd, a topless, doorless Sport Utility model, called the SSII, was introduced in 1977. The SSII could be fitted with a fabric top and doors and most left the dealership so equipped. Showing that International was serious about the SSII's purpose as a true off-road vehicle, even the base models came factory-equipped with roll bar and skid plate.

Though the SSII failed to attract many buyers, it was popular with serious off-road contenders, and specially prepared racing models competed successfully in the Baja and other off-road events.

A switch to square headlights and grid-pattern meshwork in the grille openings mark Scouts from 1980, the final production year. Because of International's need to use up its Nissan diesel inventory, nearly all 1980 Scouts are diesel-powered. *John Glancy*

The Scout 800 also offered an important drivetrain upgrade. From the extra-cost equipment list, buyers could now specify a four-speed transmission that offered more flexible power ranges for off-road use or when pulling loads. Another extra-cost option, Scouts could now be ordered with carpeting which not only gave the interior a more finished look but also helped reduce the noise level inside the vehicle.

The Scout 800 remained in production without visible changes through 1969, but an important power upgrade occurred in 1966 when a larger 196.4 cubic-inch four-cylinder engine (which had been created by lopping off one cylinder bank of International's rugged 392 V-8) became available as an option. The original 152-cubic inch four remained the standard engine with the turbocharged version continuing as an option. The larger 196.4-ci four-cylinder engine required an indent in the firewall to fit into the engine bay.

International took important steps toward providing Scout buyers with more power through turbocharging and the larger four-cylinder engine, but neither satisfied many buyers' desire that the Scout be as quick on the highway as a passenger car. The reason for this power lust is that the Scout had attracted a whole new set of buyers, as was evidenced by the fact that one-third of the vehicles being traded in on new Scouts were station wagons and sports cars.

To answer the power craving, in 1967, International added its 266-cubic inch V-8 to the Scout's growing list of engine options. By offering features, such as larger engines, that the public wanted, International opened its compact utility 4x4 to a whole new market, something which became apparent when demographic studies showed that fully half of all Scout buyers had never owned an International product.

Between 1960 and 1965, annual sales of utility four-wheel drives (predominantly Scouts and Jeeps) had grown from 11,000 to 35,000—a three-fold increase that can be largely attributed to the Scout's sales success. Industry analysts now projected annual sales of 4x4 utility vehicles topping 70,000 units

Another variation of the 1980 Scout, this one with a bright metal grille. *John Glancy*

by 1970—a whopping 700 percent increase in just one decade. Suddenly, a market that International had initially forecast it could fill with a production of just 50 units a day, loomed as a massive sales opportunity, something Ford and GM couldn't ignore. With Scout well established, its challengers had to do more than just create a Scout or Jeep clone.

Despite a shorter wheelbase that made the original Ford Bronco look boxier than the Scout, the dimensions of the two vehicles were nearly identical. Compared with the Scout's external dimensions of 68.6 inches long, 154 inches overall length, 69.2 inch height, the Bronco measured 68.8 inches wide, 152.1 inches long, and 69.2 inches high. In 1969 Chevrolet entered the 4x4 utility vehicle market with its substantially larger and more luxurious Blazer, which shared sheet metal, drivetrain, and chassis components with Chevy's full-size pickups.

International responded to the new competition largely by ignoring it. In 1969, a slightly revised 800A replaced the 800 model. Since the "new" Scout's sheet metal remained unchanged, it takes a trained eye to tell an 800 and 800A apart. Round side-marker lights replacing the former rectangular lights and square bezels around the headlights mark the most noticeable changes. Also, a slightly smaller International nameplate was now positioned lower and toward the left on the grille. One change of a consequential nature, the 800A was equipped with an energy-absorbing steering column that protected the driver from serious chest injuries in the event of a head-on crash.

For the first time Scout buyers were presented with a "limited edition" model called the Aristocrat. Through the decade of the 1970s these "limited editions," distinguished from standard Scouts by specially designed appliqués and paint schemes, became standard fare in an attempt to boost the Scout's visibility in an increasingly crowded market. Today the "limited edition" models are prized by collectors. As its name implies, the Aristocrat played to buyers wanting an upclass vehicle. In this case, "class" became a flashy metallic two-tone paint scheme and wide chrome wheels, but with more interior padding and a full carpet, the Aristocrat at least offered a quieter ride than a standard Scout.

The 800A remained essentially unchanged for two years (1969–1970). At some point during this period, the AMC 232-ci six, offered beginning in 1969 on International's light-duty 1/2-ton trucks, also became available on Scouts. The AMC six proved a good in-between engine, offering

As part of their decision to cease production of the light truck line at the end of the 1975 model year, International's management made preparations to build a longer 118-inch wheelbase Travel Top model called the Traveler that was seen as a replacement for the Travelall. The accessory-laden Traveler shown is a 1980 model. *John Glancy*

more power than the four and better gasoline mileage than the V-8.

With only the most minimal changes, in 1971 International introduced the 800B. Identifying differences of this short production model are minuscule: the marker lights have a rectangular shape, front directionals are larger, and the IH emblem is missing from the front of the hood. On the 800B, the IH emblem can be found in the lower left corner of the grille, where it replaced the International nameplate. Probably the 800B's most important feature is the optional automatic transmission which helped Scout make the transition from a working man's vehicle to a second car for active families (described in International's ads as an "Actionmobile"). Another change, most

appreciated by back seat passengers, the 800B Travel Top had larger side windows. Following the "limited edition" trend, two special 800B models, the Comanche and Snowstar—identified by special paint schemes—were offered.

One wonders why International's management didn't forgo the badge and light changes that marked the 800B. No sooner had the modestly revised Scout gotten into production than the completely redesigned Scout II appeared. The 800B didn't even last through an entire model year and you won't even see one in Scout literature unless you find a sales brochure for the 1971 models printed in late 1970 or very early 1971. The important point to note here is that the original Scout's design had been sound enough to last, with very little in the way of styling changes, for 10 years in what had become a highly competitive market.

The strong sales success of Chevrolet's Blazer clearly spelled out the criteria for the original Scout's successor. The replacement had to be larger, carry more passengers, and be more comfortable to drive, as well as quieter and smoother on the highway. Again designer Ted Ornas executed his mission well. Although the Scout II shared the original Scout's 100-inch wheelbase and overall boxy shape, the styling change was substantial. One of the most noticeable differences is the elimination of the sculpted indents on the rear quarters. A more canted windshield gave the Scout II a more streamlined look, while rounded rear corners, a forward slant to the rear of the Travel Top, and a slight inward roll on the body sides just below the beltline softened the overall styling package. From the front, a new Scout II could be recognized by a somewhat more ornate grille, consisting of three horizontal slots set inside a rectangular panel that also enclosed the headlights.

A small increase in rear overhang added about five cubic feet in interior space. This added space, combined with a lower and wider rear seat, afforded more comfort for rear passengers. The new wrapping and greater interior space appealed to buyers, and Scout II sales climbed to 30,000 in its abbreviated introductory year.

Though still a truck-style vehicle, the Scout II's option list that now included more comfortable front bucket seats and flashier looking white sidewall tires, as well as a Sport decal package, could have fit a passenger car. Extra-cost equipment making the driver's job easier included power brakes, power steering, and an automatic transmission. Air conditioning assured driver and passenger comfort, even in the warmest climates, while automatic front hubs provided four-wheel-drive traction for snow covered or rain glazed pavement without the driver's having to stop the vehicle and manually engage the front drive axles.

Engine choices remained the same as those available with the 800B: the 196 ci four, the 232 ci AMC six, and the 304 V-8 plus International's 345 ci V-8. The big 345 V-8 had been added for buyers who wanted to use their Scout II as a towing vehicle for boats and travel trailers. Bigger brakes improved safety, particularly given the new Scout's more powerful engines, while a wider choice of axle ratios helped buyers tailor their Scouts to off-road operation or highway cruising.

The Scout II remained unchanged for 1972, except that Scouts sold in California were not available with the four-cylinder engine due to that state's increasingly stringent emissions standards. A slight modification to the grille identified the 1973 models. Changes to the grille structure consisted of a center divider and vertical bars. Federal emissions standards now required that engines in cars and light-duty trucks be operated on unleaded gasoline. In the process of meeting this and other environmental standards, International, along with other manufacturers, detuned its engines, making them less efficient. Engines of this vintage are not only dogs in the power department but also have the fuel appetite of a fighter jet.

No visible changes marked the 1974 and 1975 models, though International continued to expand the Scout's special decal and equipment packages. An oil embargo that had followed the 1973 Yom Kippur Arab-Israeli war resulted in long lines at the pumps and a nationwide threat of gasoline rationing. A 300 percent increase in gasoline prices over a one-year period sent the public scrambling for vehicles offering high fuel mileage and left gas guzzling rigs like V-8-powered Scouts sitting stagnant on the sales lots. To help revive sales, International brought back the 196-ci slant four. Overall buyer response was dismal, and Scout sales for 1974 hit a low of only 6,714 units.

In 1975, with fuel prices stabilized and memories of the long lines at the gasoline pumps quickly fading, Americans returned to buying the V-8-powered vehicles they preferred. Although the slant four remained the base engine, over 82 percent of all Scouts sold in 1975 were equipped with a V-8. Since there seemed little reason to continue offering the AMC six, this engine quietly vanished from the option list. A sense that the comfortable life to which Americans were accustomed had returned sent Scout sales surging to 21,366 units.

As part of the decision to cease production of the light-truck line at the end of the 1975 model year, International's management made preparations to build a longer 118-inch wheelbase Scout that could be set up either as a pickup (short cap) or passenger wagon (long cap). In pickup form the new, long wheelbase Scout was called the Terra. With a cargo bed measuring a full six feet in length, the Terra offered the hauling capacity of a short-box pickup, plus the traction advantages of four-wheel drive. It was a nice looking package that garnered strong first-year sales of 15,732 units. The long wheelbase

Travel Top model was called the Traveler, a clear pitch to former Travelall buyers. With a more spacious interior than the standard Scout II, plus a convenient rear liftgate/tailgate, the Traveler helped boost Scout II sales (minus Terra production) to a new high of 25,840 units.

A Scout first, for 1976 buyers could option a high-quality, diesel engine built by Nissan. Although buyers of heavy-duty trucks are well familiar with a diesel engine's advantages, including long life and low maintenance, International relied on rising gasoline prices and the diesel's reputation for fuel economy to sell the diesel option in the Scout market. In the mid-1970s, diesel fuel could still be purchased for about half the cost per gallon of gasoline.

Although the Nissan diesel had a small 198-cubic inch displacement and produced only 82 horsepower, the engine's inherent high torque made it a gutsy motor that excelled in any working setting, from driving off road to pulling a boat or travel trailer. *Four Wheeler* magazine was so impressed with the performance and economy of the Scout/Nissan diesel combination that in 1976, it tapped the Scout Traveler with the Nissan diesel for its coveted "Four Wheeler of the Year" award. International would continue to offer the Nissan diesel through the end of Scout production in 1980.

To honor the America's bicentennial the Scout offered two special trim models called the "Spirit of '76" and the "Patriot." Essentially identical in appearance, both featured red and blue side trim on a Winter White body with the interior upholstered in Wedgewood Blue vinyl. With the "Spirit" package buyers also got a blue denim fabric top, a sport steering wheel, roll bar, chrome wheels, and Goodyear "Tracker AT"

10 x 15 tires. Authentic "Spirit Scouts" are extremely rare as only 384 were manufactured. The "Spirit" package can be authenticated by the Spirit appliqué code number 10876 on the options list and "Spirit 76" handwritten on the line setting ticket. "Patriot" Scouts have the same "Spirit" markings and special equipment, but are fitted with a metal top. "Patriots" were built in long wheelbase Terra and Traveler configurations, as well as standard wheelbase Scout IIs. It is believed that only one Terra, seven Travelers, and 50 Scout II "Patriots" were built. These are rare Scouts indeed!

A new grille, consisting of two horizontally oriented rectangular openings inside a bright metal frame, marked the 1977 models. To appeal to the off-roading crowd, a topless, doorless Sport Utility model, called the SSII, was introduced; it came standard-equipped with both roll bar and skid plate. The SSII could be fitted with a fabric top and doors and most were so equipped. Though this rugged-looking Scout failed to attract many buyers, it was popular with serious off-road contenders and specially prepared racing models competed successfully in the Baja and other off-road events. For 1977 Scout sales rose to 39,382 units.

The easiest way to recognize a 1978 Scout is by the width of the bright metal frame around the grille openings, which is slightly thicker than in 1977. Sales fell slightly to 39,191. No change of note occurred for 1979, through sales climbed to 44,343.

A switch to square headlights and grid-pattern meshwork in the grille openings mark Scouts from 1980, the final production year. Because of International's need to use up its Nissan diesel inventory, nearly all 1980 Scouts are diesel-powered. (See accompanying chart.)

Other Scout engines, the V-8s and the slant four, could be used in other products, but the Nissan diesel had only one application: the Scout. Some of the Nissan diesels were equipped with turbochargers, an option that made a diesel-powered Scout quite a lively vehicle. Other changes included four-wheel drive and power steering as standard equipment, an 85-mile per hour speedometer, satin-finish black trim on the vent window and door glass frames, and a smaller 15-inch diameter steering wheel. Several side-trim appliqués could be optioned, including Rally stripes, a side spear, the See-Thru Flare, and woodgrain trim on Traveler models.

Nissan Diesel Engined Scout Production

Year	Engine	Production
1976	SD633	1602
1977	SD633	1038
1978	SD633	1045
1979	SD633	537
	SD633 Turbo	1108
1980	SD633	5389
Total		10,182

For its final year, Scout sales dropped to 30,059, largely attributable to a decrease in advertising and the fear of owning an orphan that makes buyers shy away from soon-to-be-discontinued products.

Even as the Scout was fading into history, its original designer, Ted Ornas, was trying to sell International management on a new-generation Scout that would use weight-saving composite body construction and be offered in three platform variations. The three vehicles would be called the "Sports Enthusiast," an off-road version on a 100-inch wheelbase with full-time four-wheel drive and a new lightweight engine: target weight, 2800 pounds; the "Family Cruiser," an all-round recreational vehicle with four-wheel drive for highway and leisure off-road; and the "Scout Van," a Travelall-type vehicle built on a 118-inch wheelbase to accommodate up to eight passengers, designed with front-wheel drive and a rear module for four-wheel drive: target weight, 3200 pounds.

This composite-based concept series was a decade ahead of its time. Sadly, lack of financial resources and management support resulted in only one prototype being built, a Sports Enthusiast model, code SSV. This experimental Scout-of-the-future still exists and can be seen in the Auburn Museum in Auburn, Indiana.

On October 21, 1980, the last Scout rolled off the Fort Wayne assembly line. The Scout's demise traces to a number of factors: absence of a dealership network attuned to selling light-duty, utility-type vehicles, advertising that ignored women, who had become major force in new vehicle purchase decisions, and a long and bitter strike between IH workers and management that hampered new product development. Rather than lament the Scout's passing, perhaps it's better to focus on what the Scout accomplished. Within months of its introduction the Scout had become International's all-time best selling vehicle, and in so-doing pioneered the multi-purpose vehicle concept later copied by Ford's Bronco and Chevy's Blazer. The Scout also made important technological advances by introducing small diesels to the automotive market, and in the pioneering development work toward the concept, Scout foresaw by at least 20 years the widespread use of composites in vehicle construction. No doubt about it, with the Scout International had hit the target on the bull's eye, first try.

chapter thirteen

INTERNATIONAL'S MEDIUM AND HEAVY-DUTY TRUCKS:
A Historical Overview

International waited until 1915 to introduce its first in what today would be called the medium-duty field. The Model G, offered in what is descriptively called the "Slope Hood" line, had a 1-ton load rating and used a four-cylinder, 4x5 engine from the 8-16 International tractor. Due to its ability to carry a larger payload, the Model G turned out to be the best selling truck in the Slope Hood series, selling 11,000 copies between 1915 and 1923.

Certainly International wasn't the first truck builder to offer a model with a load rating larger than 1 ton. Numerous other makes had been building trucks in the medium and even heavy-duty load classes almost from the "get-go." As early as 1905, Mack offered a 50-horsepower, 5-ton truck. But the market for heavy haulers had been limited due to lack of improved roads, the widespread use of bone-jarring solid-rubber tires which had the additional drawback of poor traction, and chain drive. Progress, both in highway construction and in tire development and metallurgy would be needed for larger load rating trucks to be used for other than work-site (as in mining or construction) or short-haul purposes. By 1915, sufficient progress had been made in each crucial area to account for the Model G's success.

In the S series, International expanded its medium and heavy-duty truck lines through a whole range of models. Shown here is a 1929 S-26, a 1-ton rated truck equipped with a six-cylinder engine that was built to serve as a medium-duty model. The example shown here is owned by Bob Brown, who has entered his meticulously restored truck in the Great American Race.

Riding on pneumatic tires, the Model G was driveshaft driven, a combination that allowed a smoother ride (the concern with ride quality was more for the longevity of the truck and condition of the load than for the comfort of the driver) without the frequent lubrication and adjustment required by chain drive. Also in 1915, International introduced the 3 1/2-ton rated Model L, its largest capacity truck, using solid rubber tires.

In 1921, the Model G became the Model 61 and its load rating was boosted to 3-ton. Likewise, the Model L became the 101 with a 5-ton rating.

Under the S series, International expanded its medium-duty truck models with the Model 43, a 2-tonner, the Model 63 with a 3-ton rating, and the Model 94 with a 4 1/2-ton load rating. A 10-ton rated Model 103, basically a stretched wheelbase 94, was also offered. As with the Model L/61, the Model 63 proved to be the best seller with 10,000 built between 1924 and 1927. All three models used the same 4 1/2 x 5 engine and had shaft drive. As before, models with the largest load ratings used solid rubber tires. Tire technology had not yet developed to the point where pneumatic tires could bear heavy weights.

Medium-duty D-series trucks, like the D-30 shown here, were popular with fire departments. Today a retired fire truck makes a very desirable collector piece.

With the A line, International increased the load limit of its largest capacity model to 10 tons. Powering the new line of medium and heavy-duty trucks were more powerful Lycoming six-cylinder engines. Another important technical development was introduced in 1927, when International offered its A6, A7, and A8 models with a double-reduction rear axle. As the name implies, a double-reduction axle contains two sets of gears as

The combination of vertical grille and bold cycle style fenders give International's larger K and KB-series trucks a brute force appearance that most collectors find appealing. Although the post-war KB models retained virtually identical appearance with the earlier K series, numerous improvements developed during the war were incorporated into the later models. The truck seen here is a 1949 KB-6.

Although International discontinued its light-duty R series in 1955, several of the larger models remained in production until 1961. The medium-duty models remained popular with fire departments.

opposed to a single set in a normal, single-reduction rear axle. To see the advantage of double reduction, let's look at how the gear ratio is determined in a single reduction rear axle. With single reduction the drive pinion (a beveled gear which is attached to the end of the driveshaft) engages the differential ring gear. The ratio between the number of teeth on the drive pinion and ring gear determines the gearing ratio. For example, if there are 9 teeth on the pinion and 37 teeth on the ring gear, then the truck has a rear axle ratio of 4.1 to 1. Said another way, the driveshaft spins 4.1 times to each 1 revolution of the rear axles. One of the reasons that International offered a double reduction rear axle is a medium or heavy-duty truck needs a large numerical differential ratio. To achieve the necessary reduction, the ring gear needs not only to be large, but also the entire torque of the engine is applied against one pair of gears which engage on a lateral mesh. Two problems arise from this. First, the large ring gear also requires a larger rear axle "pumpkin" which lowers

the truck's ground clearance. Second, applying all the engine torque against the single ring and pinion gearset increases the risk of stripping or damaging the gears, especially given metallurgy limitations of the 1920s.

The double reduction rear axle addressed both problems while offering a further benefit that helped extend the longevity of trucks so equipped. With double reduction, the ring gear does not directly turn the axle shafts as is the condition in most single reduction axles. Instead, the ring gear spins a second gear set that turns the axle shafts. It is this combination of gear sets that gives the double-reduction axle its name. Because two sets of gears are used to multiply the final drive ratio, the size of the "pumpkin" in the rear axle is reduced, increasing ground clearance. The third benefit comes from the truck's weight being supported by the axle housing and not the drive mechanism. This design, in which the axle housing supports the weight of the truck and its load, is called a "full floating" axle. Double reduction rear axles

International's medium-duty Loadstar trucks of the 1960s were extremely popular and a particular favorite of farmers. The retired grain truck shown here now serves as a maintenance vehicle for a summer camp.

remained an option on International heavy-duty trucks into the K and KB series of the 1940s.

When the C series appeared in 1934, International introduced its first cabover models, designated the C-300. This "pug nose" short wheelbase truck was designed for the tighter turning radius required to maneuver narrow inner city streets and alleys. Moving the front wheels back underneath the driver's seat and eliminating the traditional long hood enabled International's engineers to shrink the C-300 wheelbase to 99 inches on models fitted with an 11-foot cargo body and 117 inches on the 15-foot cargo body version. Typical purchasers of these cabover models were beverage distributors and delivery businesses like Railway Express.

Other significant developments included improved tires and the experimental use of diesel engines. Long-distance truck transport required pneumatic tires that could stand up under heavy loads. Tires with a load rating of 2,000 pounds finally appeared in 1933, allowing International to fit even its heaviest-duty C-series trucks with pneumatic tires. Cummins diesels were installed in a small number of C-50 models to test the reliability of the new engines, as well as to form a basis of evaluation as to the advantages of diesel power.

The 1937 D series brought not only fresh styling, but also an expanded line of six-wheel models for use in such heavy hauling settings as mining, construction, and timber hauling. Trucks in this range had load carrying capability of up to 30 tons and were largely diesel powered. Although styling was certainly a hallmark of International's D models, the medium-duty D-300

A pair of International tractors. As seen on the left, International also built its Loadstar trucks in cabover configurations. These shorter wheelbase trucks were often used where cargo drop-off had to be made at congested inner city locations.

cabovers changed little in appearance from their C-series counterparts; improvements were made in engine insulation to reduce engine noise and heat that had been causes of complaint by operators of the C-series models.

For the K series, which appeared in 1940, International departed from the practice established in 1929 with the A line of using a single cab design on all its trucks, light to heavy-duty. Light- and medium-duty K-series trucks, up to the K-5 model, wore re-styled cabs that can be recognized by a less rounded contour on the rear of the roof and a higher ledge for the door windows. The K-6 and larger trucks continued to use the D-series cab, which blended very well with the K line's simpler, more rugged looking grille and overall frontal design.

For the heavier duty K-6 through 12 models, International developed a more powerful valve-in-head gasoline engine. Stronger gearboxes and axles complemented the higher powered engines. As might be expected from previous sales patterns, the most popular model among International's trucks in the medium and heavy-duty range was the K-5. This truck with its 15,000-pound rating was very popular with farmers for a number of

reasons: its strong construction and reliability, its overall handsome styling, and the availability of several wheelbase lengths as well as a two-speed rear axle. The K-5 was also an ideal size for smaller fire departments, and many were purchased for use as tankers, pumpers, and ladder trucks. Collectors who have been able to acquire a retired K-series fire truck are indeed fortunate as these trucks are typically very low mileage and well cared for.

During World War II, International was called upon to produce trucks for the military in large volumes. Although International supplied military trucks in several sizes and configurations, from a volume standpoint its main model was the M-5-6 2 1/2-ton 6x6. Military specifications called for trucks with front-drive axles, a feature International lacked experience building but quickly implemented, using Eaton differentials for the front axle. The transfer case and rear axles were International's own design. A 6x4 version without the front drive axle, designated the M-5-6, was also built for use primarily by the Army. The typical body configuration was as a cargo truck, but short wheelbase dump trucks, tractors, and wreckers were also built. International shared

International's Transtar distance-hauling trucks carried a large share of the nation's freight in the decades of the 1970s and 1980s.

production of 2 1/2-ton trucks in the 6x6 configuration with GMC and Studebaker.

When production of civilian trucks resumed, International mildly restyled its K models as the new KB line. On light-duty up to KB-5 models, an extension of the chrome ribs at the bottom of the grille served as the major appearance difference. The KB-5 remained a best-selling model, with just under 64,000 built between 1947 and 1949. From an appearance standpoint, the KB-6 and larger trucks remained unchanged, although

these trucks incorporated many engineering improvements that resulted from wartime production. Among the most striking of the KB models was the KB-8, which was painted an eye-catching combination of red frame and wheels, black running boards, fenders, and bumper, and cab, hood, and grille in a body color selected from eight choices. Powering the KB-8 was International's solidly engineered 360-cubic inch Red Diamond engine, the powerplant used in the military M-5H-6. Tandem rear axles, another feature that had

By the C series, International trucks were being fitted as school busses to transport children to centralized schools. These photos taken in the Lake Ontario region of Upstate New York illustrate the challenge of maintaining a school schedule in winter weather.

seen refinement as a result of International's experience building military trucks, was also available on K- and KB-6 and larger models. Trucks equipped with the tandem rear axle received a special designation, as in K-6-F or KB-6-F.

In the late 1940s and 1950s, because of the long distances and relatively sparse traffic, several western states established special regulations for long-distance trucks that allowed longer trailers and heavier loads than were permitted on the highways in other parts of the country. Several manufacturers, including International, built trucks specifically for these western highway regulations. The plant where these special West Coast trucks were built was located in Emeryville, California. The appearance of these W-series models (more commonly called Emeryville trucks) was quite unlike trucks in the KB series being built at Springfield and Fort Wayne. The cab was wider and had angular lines, as opposed to the rounded contours of the D/K-KB cabs. Engines included Cummins diesels, as well as International's largest gasoline or diesel power-plants. Customers could select transmissions and rear axles from several manufacturer's components, including Eaton and Spicer. In this sense, Emeryville trucks were built largely to customer specifications, a common practice with large trucks, but a new concept when International developed it. The Emeryville plant remained in operation until 1968, when the plant was closed and production was moved to a newer, larger plant in San Leandro, California.

With the advent of the L and R series in the early 1950s, the number of variants within International's truck lines expanded so dramatically that over 1,500 different truck versions were claimed to be available. In 1956, International added powerful V-8 engines, equipped to run on either gasoline or LPG. In the 1960s, International began designating its various medium and heavy-duty trucks as different "star" series. The medium-duty models now wore the Loadstar designation, while heavier duty models were grouped in the Transtar or Fleetstar categories. The Loadstar line continued the popularity of International's earlier medium-duty lines.

By the 1970s, International was building medium and heavy-duty trucks in practically every marketable configuration, including cabover tractors and snubnosed straight models. Other nonconventional compact cab models were built to accommodate expanded cargo requirements. International's medium and heavy-duty truck lines were expanding to fill practically every niche in the industry, and based on model proliferation, the company seemed to dominate the industry. But within, the manufacturing empire known as International Harvester was crumbling, and it would take a complete restructuring, combined with a new name, to bring about the company's renaissance.

CLUB ADDRESSES

IH Collectors
684 N. Northwest Hwy, Box 250
Park Ridge, IL 60068

Scout & International Truck Assoc.
P.O. Box 12
Ogden, IL 61859

Antique Truck Historical Society (ATHS)
P.O. Box 531168
Birmingham, AL 35223

Antique Truck Club of America (ATCA)
P.O. Box 291
Hershey, PA 17033

INDEX